The Long Winter

One Man's Journey Through the
Darkness of Foster Care

Paul L. Owen

authorHOUSE®

AuthorHouse™
1663 Liberty Drive
Bloomington, IN 47403
www.authorhouse.com
Phone: 1-800-839-8640

First published by AuthorHouse 8/6/2010

ISBN: 978-1-4520-4873-4 (sc)
ISBN: 978-1-4520-4874-1 (e)
ISBN: 978-1-4520-4872-7 (hc)

Library of Congress Control Number: 2010910089

Printed in the United States of America
Bloomington, Indiana

This book is printed on acid-free paper.

"When my father and my mother forsake me, then the LORD will take me up" (Psalm 27:10).

Another difficult but rewarding academic year has come to an end. I am walking back from the registrar's office, where I have gratefully filed the last of my paperwork. It's May in the Blue Ridge Mountains of North Carolina, and now I'm a free man until August. The temperature is warm but mild, and there is a light breeze blowing as I walk across campus and enter the idyllic stone building that houses my office at Montreat College.

The students and most of the faculty are gone now. Apart from me, the building is empty. I sit at my desk and begin to sort through some e-mails, but my heart is not in it for some reason. I feel strangely distracted and despondent. I look out my window towards the parking lot and the mountain scenery beyond. The trees on the nearby ridges are glowing in the late afternoon sun. An intangible calm in the air is signaling the transition from spring to the lazy months of summer.

After a few minutes of clicking on my keyboard I sit back in my chair for a stretch, then pull off my glasses and rub my eyes. Sitting up straight in my chair again, I reach over and shut off the computer.

The last two weeks have been a hectic marathon of final exams and grading papers. The constant pressures of lecturing, department chair duties and committee work have taken their toll this year, and for some reason I'm acutely aware of the advance of time. My life is passing so quickly these days. I'm definitely showing signs of age. Hints of grey are beginning to show in my beard and along my temples, and there is a new weariness in my bones that I could not have imagined in my 20's.

My work is done for the year and as often happens when I have more time on my hands than I am accustomed to, I feel a growing sense of melancholy gripping me, wrapping me in its cold embrace. It's as though I have been running from something for a good while, and as I pause to catch my breath, it catches up to me.

"Thirty-seven years old," I think to myself. "That's how old *she was* when I was born."

And now I am alone, in a way that runs deeper than the empty offices and hallways of my quiet building. At times like this I feel isolated in a daunting world. My thoughts turn to a mother long gone and distant years of foster homes. My lips tighten, my chest contracts, as I return to people, places and experiences that I keep safely buried in the deep wells of my most distant memory.

I am thirteen years old again. It's November 5, 1983 in the Upper Snake River Valley of Idaho. On that day, as the inhabitants of Idaho Falls stir from their beds, rub the sleep from their eyes and face a new day, I face a *new world*. A world in which my mother is gone forever. I am left behind to face the same challenges which confront hundreds of thousands of children in American society today, who pass through our midst with no family to call their own.

My father died of cancer when I was five. After that, my mother did the best she could to take care of me, but was plagued with physical and mental troubles that made her own life difficult. I had no idea at the time how her death would propel me down dark paths, crisscrossing the American continent, and experiencing first-hand the vulnerability, abuse and neglect of so many children who are swept headlong into the bubbling currents of an indifferent system.

At the age of thirteen, on my first official day as an orphan in America, I began to learn harsh lessons. Lessons about the realities of life, human nature, and the challenge of living on the fringes of society. My experiences taught me how to survive when life offered me neither security nor identity. In a world structured around the foundation of stable families and parental guidance, it was up to me to carve out a place of safety and meaning.

As I gaze out the window on this late spring afternoon, the trees still ablaze with glorious sun, I return to those difficult years. I relive the experiences that led me to this moment. From the quiet shelter of my office, I play again in my mind the events that led me to this life, the path that I took to get here.

The Early Years (1970-1976)

I was born in September 1970 in a sprawling mid-sized town in Idaho called Pocatello. I suppose, or, I guess I hope, that's an Indian word for something. For me the "Indian" (in the Native American sense) is a symbol of the past, back when the world still made sense, before human progress suffocated our spirits. The world of those who lived close to nature, lonely and isolated, yet fully alive, like monks waking up early for prayer.

Whenever I think of Pocatello, the place of my own beginnings, it is always winter in my mind. I am in an automobile, and someone else is driving. I hear the voice of Uncle Norman commenting on how dirty the air is now, with all the pollution and growth.

"Nope. It wasn't ever this aways when I was growin' up."

I stare out the window. To the right, freeway exits and homes of various sizes come and go quickly. That's where the people are, in their warm houses, sitting around kitchen tables, children busy with homework. Fathers sit in recliner chairs, watching TV with glazed expressions, while dogs sleep on the carpet with their feet in the air.

To the left are hills, covered with sagebrush and snow, inviting us to hear their wordless witness to a simpler past, still remembered by the sad mountains in the distance. I see mountain men, Mormon settlers, Indian tribes camped by riverbeds, smoke from their campfires reaching upward, like priestly hands lifted in prayer, wolves and grizzlies still roaming about the land.

Somehow in the late 1960's, my mother and father, Leona Jardine and Leon Owen, met in Pocatello. My mother told me that they both worked at Deseret Industries, a kind of Mormon used-goods shopping center. Perhaps they worked some shifts together, and he nervously offered to buy her lunch one day.

"Sure, that would be quite nice," she replies, with a tight-lipped smile and a nod.

You can buy most anything at the "D.I.," from toys, to clothes, to kitchenware, to furniture, and washers and dryers. All at a discounted price, courtesy of the Mormon social machine. My mom took me there once, when I was very young, and told me that is where she first met my dad.

Looking pensive, she remembered, "He was a very sweet man."

For that reason, the location became a kind of sacred space for me, a place to visit when my father was gone, and I would search for connections to him. Connections at all.

On one occasion, years later when I was growing up in Idaho Falls, I came out of the D.I., where I had been wandering the aisles with no money to spend, into the heat of an Idaho summer. The sun was bearing down like a furnace as I exited the cool interior of the spacious building. I could smell the nearby pavement, the grass and the trees. My senses were bombarded by sprinklers, houses, buildings, and cars on busy streets. I had nowhere to go, no place that required my childish presence on a summer day.

As I wandered about in no particular direction, I can remember finding a bag of barbequed pork rinds on the grass beside the parking lot. Like a pirate with a newly discovered treasure, I sat in the grass and devoured every last one of them. I felt masculine and content, like a young hunter-gatherer, living off the land.

My earliest memory though, comes from an earlier time when I was still living in Pocatello with my mom and dad. I am very young, young enough to eat in a baby chair. I am in a room, a basement, and alone. This frightens me, and I begin to cry loudly. Around me, on the walls, are cans of food. I look at those stacks of cans, not knowing who or what they are. Years later, I was shown pictures of myself as a baby, in just such a room, with the cans on the shelves. Whether it was taken on that occasion I do not know. But in my first conscious memory, I am abandoned by my parents, left to the custody of cans and silent walls.

Next thing I know, I am riding with my aunt Bonnie in her car. There she sits, with her reddish hair, and her country clothes, a resolute look on her face as she steers. Someone had decided that my mom was not able to take care of me. I know she went to an insane asylum (as they called it back then), and that may be the reason I lived with my aunt and uncle. Or maybe that was the reason she went insane.

Leona Owen had a challenging life. A high fever during her infancy left her severely handicapped on her left side, affecting her leg and her arm. She walked with a pronounced limp, and the fingers on her left hand were shriveled into something like a clenched fist, extending uselessly from the end of her deformed arm, scarred from childhood surgeries at the Mayo clinic which did her no good.

She was confronted from the beginning with obstacles too strong to conquer. She would never finish high school, never learn to drive a car, or pursue a career. Her charitable employment with the Deseret Industries where she met my dad was the only job she ever had. Providence had cut her off at every turn, frustrating every hope, every plan and dream. She must have accepted early on that she would never travel to distant lands, never achieve noteworthy accomplishments, or gain the attention of a society that is only interested in those who succeed.

So for whatever reason, when I was very young, I lived for a while with my aunt Bonnie and my uncle Norman out in the country, in Menan, Idaho. A quiet land of fences, fields and old country homes with big grassy yards and trampolines. Mormon families mostly, with wholesome breakfast tables, hard-working dads, dull routines and buried secrets. Mothers hang clothes on the wire as little children play on the lawn. Labrador retrievers bark and chase cars along gravel roads, for reasons known only to themselves.

I am driving with Aunt Bonnie to the local store, which is a great adventure. It's one of those small country stores, where people go to buy odds and ends and seek the presence of familiar faces. It must have been summer, as the weather is hot, and my bare legs are sticking to the seat of the car as I fiddle with my seatbelt. I am full of excitement as we arrive.

As she closes the car door behind me she warns, "Now don't you run off little mister. You stick next to me. And don't touch anything."

We walk through the tall aisles of canned goods and boxes, and Bonnie buys me a bottled orange soda. As we return home, the warm summer air blows into the car, and my senses are full of hay and grass and contentment. A woman sings on the radio. Her enchanting voice is sealed forever on my memory. She is singing the melody in my head as I type.

"I beg your pardon, I never promised you a rose garden . . ."

"Aunt Bonnie, what's a rose garden?"

"It means that we don't always get the things we want in life," she muses. She doesn't look my way, and seems lost in thoughts of her own.

Eventually my mom got me back. And the next thing I remember is walking hand in hand with her to the local A&W. By this time my dad has taken ill with cancer, and is enduring a miserable death at the veterans' hospital in Salt Lake City. (One of the handful of things I do know about my dad is that he was a veteran of World War II and the Korean War.) My mom purchases a root beer float for me when we arrive at our destination. I feel loved and protected as we sit there together, just the two of us against the world.

I can still see the seat I am sitting on. It is a stool with a swiveling red seat, with a counter in front, looking out the window onto the busy boulevard. Cars pass by on the way to their various destinations, scarcely giving the two of us a second's thought. I wonder what was going through her mind as she sat there next to me, watching her son grip an icy mug with his little hands, full of root beer and ice cream and a mother's love?

Some months later I am ill with bronchitis, and a doctor has come to visit our apartment. He is older, dressed in a formal way, with suspenders, and carries a black bag. I remember finding it difficult to pronounce the name of the illness, and the doctor commenting with a chuckle that it is an awfully big word for a child my age. The doctor talks with an optimistic tone about the upcoming school year, when I will attend a *full day* of classes, not a just a half day like kindergarten. The thought causes me no small amount of anxiety about the future, mixed with childish excitement.

I enjoyed visiting with the old doctor, and soaked up his attention. "Open wide," he orders, as he looks down my throat. "That's a good man." He was kind and fatherly, and carried himself with a wholesome air.

He reminded me of the doctor on *Little House on the Prairie*, the prism through which I interpreted the world and all my experiences in those days. The show was an image of the way the world is supposed to be, captured and preached every week on our small, black and white TV screen. A safe world in which fathers are always there, firm but kind, full of wisdom, always working hard to take care of the family. Communities that gather around the weak and the unfortunate, caring for them when the chips are down. A dreamy alternative existence, full of teachers and doctors and preachers who each in their own way make the world a better place to live.

The one-story apartment building we lived in at the time was humble by any standards. It was a converted home that had been broken into apartments. We had no bedroom. I slept on a cot in the kitchen, while my mom slept in the living room on the couch. Our landlord thought himself a theologian of sorts. I once asserted in his presence that Jesus had lived his whole life without a single sin (having recently learned that point of theology in Sunday school at the Mormon Church).

The landlord-divine corrected me. "Jesus *did* sin *once*," he said in a low tone. He then gravely informed me that when Jesus was about to go to the cross, he sinned against God by trying to escape his divinely appointed fate. Jesus lost his nerve and tried to avoid doing God's will. He had a very somber look on his face as he passed on to me this secret *gnosis*. I stood corrected, and made a mental note to be more discerning in the assessment of my Sunday school lessons from that time forward.

When I brought up the point to my teacher the following Sunday at church, she was not receptive to my critically-enlightened views. This same landlord also let me in on the little-known secret of his own true identity. He just happened to be the brother of Michael Landon from *Little House on the Prairie*. I was so impressed! It never occurred to me that he might not be telling the truth.

The absence of my father left a gap that my mom tried to fill by contacting the local chapter of the Big Brother organization. The Big Brother appointed to me was a tall, friendly black man with an afro, who drove a big blue van with a mural of some sort on the window, as was popular in those days. He and his girlfriend, a thin woman with long, straight, blond hair and a pleasant disposition, took me to McDonald's for the first time in my life. They ordered me a hamburger, presumably a Big Mac, and laughed playfully at my attempts to fit my small mouth around the bun.

"That's a pretty big burger isn't it little guy?" my Big Brother said with a smile and a chuckle, his arm resting in a fatherly way across my shoulders. I nodded in agreement as I opened my mouth as wide as possible and tried to chew a path through the interior of the juicy burger.

Sometimes my Big Brother took me home with him for overnight stays. One time I was tucked into bed when someone that I did not recognize appeared at the door. I was laying there in the bed falling asleep, clothed only in my underwear, when the strange man suddenly showed up and entered the room.

"Hey Paul," he said as he stepped towards me. "I thought you might like some company." He sat down on the bed and continued to talk. He spoke with a gentle, soothing voice, attempting to put me at ease as he stroked my hair, and then reached over and uncovered me from underneath the blankets. I was bewildered, looking up at him with blue, five-year old eyes, as he stroked my cheek and began to touch my bare skin with his fingertips.

He began to kiss me, first on the cheeks, then on the lips.

"Come on, it's okay. I won't hurt you baby."

I found it hard to breathe as he covered my small lips with his own and forced his wet tongue into my mouth, his saliva choking my throat. I felt like I was suffocating. My memory hides the details. Emptiness and melancholy. The next day I am returned home to my mother, quiet perhaps, not quite myself. I don't remember any more visits to my Big Brother's house, but questions linger to this day. Where on earth was he, and why was I left alone in his house with a strange man?

My dad died of breast cancer around that time. Shortly before his death, we went down to visit him at the VA hospital in Salt Lake City. I can recall very little of that brief encounter, my sole memory of him. I do remember at one point, talking back to my mom for some reason, and that my dad sternly instructed me not to talk to her that way.

"Look me in the eye. Do you understand?"

"Yes," I nod my small head, looking up at him like a god.

What was it like for him to look at his little boy, knowing that was the last time he would see me on this earth? What went through his mind as he held me in his arms, lingering in that moment, before he watched me walk away, holding my mother's hand as I looked back at him? And what was it that he whispered in my ear, as he kissed my cheek before putting me down?

I can almost remember.

Then, like some passing dream in the middle of the night, he was gone. I have the faintest glimmer of my mother receiving the news of his death in our gloomy little apartment. I remember nothing at all of his funeral in July, though I am told it was very hot, so hot that one of the soldiers assigned to participate in the ceremony fainted from sunstroke.

Growing Up in Idaho Falls (1976-1979)

My childhood years may have been challenging, but I thought little of it at the time. We stayed in that little apartment for about two years, through my first grade at Hawthorne Elementary. I remember next to nothing of that time, apart from the names of my rotund kindergarten teacher, Ms. Daily, followed by Mrs. Ingram in the first grade. I do vividly recall one school lesson, in which we were introduced to the alphabet through colorful characters associated with each letter. "P" (for Paul) was a very cute porcupine. I was so proud when the time came for the character representing my letter to come onto the screen. The "P" character gave me a sense of identity, a sense of place, in the bewildering world of elementary school.

It is during this period that Ruth Hudson entered the picture. She was a distant cousin of my mother through her own mother's side of the family. A busty woman in her fifties, whose face bore stern expressions, Ruth was devoutly Roman Catholic, and thus never really fit in with the mainstream of my mother's Mormon family. My mother's family was very proud of our pioneer roots, and our direct descent from the

Prophet Brigham Young and his first wife. In the absence of a father figure, she seemed to take the role of a disciplinarian when the occasion called for it.

Once, when I was five or six, she caught me smoking cigarettes with the neighborhood children. I can think of nothing more natural for a little boy to do with his friends on a summer day. As a remedy, Ruth made me inhale the smoke of one of the cigarettes until I vomited. She towers above me still, sticking the smoking instrument of torture into my mouth.

"Go ahead, breathe it in. Deeper. It's not so fun now, is it mister?" But truth be told, it *was* worth it. Cigarettes have an almost irresistible attraction for little boys.

By the time the second grade rolled around, we had moved. Perhaps the landlord had raised the rent, or maybe it's just that Ruth found an affordable place for us to live where there was a bedroom for my mother to sleep. In any event, we relocated to a different part of town, populated by Mexican immigrants. For the first time I became conscious of these people, who seemed to keep to themselves, and spoke a strange language. Sometimes I would play with their children. That was when I first learned to ride a bike (a birthday present from Aunt Marie and Uncle Howard) without training wheels. It was a neighborly Mexican who took the training wheels off, and helped me learn to ride on the road by pushing me along.

"There you go. You will go a lot faster without this thing slowing you down," he says as he stands the bike upright and directs me to the handlebars. I stare at my new ride with a mixture of fear and eager energy. I was about to straddle across the back of a wild tiger. A mustang. Something dangerous.

"Now just hold the handles steady and point the tire where you want it to go," he encourages as he holds one handlebar and pushes on my back to increase my speed. Then suddenly, he is no longer with me, and I am moving down the street with a new-found power of motion. Now I can take myself wherever I want to be.

Where is that man now I wonder? I can see him in some quiet neighborhood, somewhere out west, watching his grandchildren play from a comfortable seat. Sipping a drink and glancing in my direction, as though he senses the presence of my thoughts.

I have brief memories of those years. We lived in two different apartments along the same street in the period spanning second and third grade. The street dead-ended at the railroad tracks that ran north and south through the middle of town. I was very conscious of those tracks and the mystery they held. I was vaguely aware that if you followed the tracks for long enough, they would take you to far away places. From time to time, when feeling adventurous, I would follow them quite a ways to the north or south, for an hour or two, until I lost my nerve and retraced my steps toward home.

I associated the tracks with a race of men known as "hobos." Hobos had a glorious life, riding the trains around the country and stopping to camp wherever the scenery pleased them. I envied them intensely, and secretly wished some day to join them on their journeys. I never did meet one of them along the tracks, or even see them sitting in the trains enjoying the ride, but I just knew they had to be there inside the cars, perhaps hiding from my alert gaze.

Friday and Saturday evenings were special times. One of my fascinations was monsters, and on the weekends my mother always let me sleep on the living room couch instead of in the kitchen on my cot. Covered with a cheap old blanket decorated with colorful little animals my mom had sewn onto it, I would lie on the couch and stay up late, intermittently dozing and waking to check the time, while I waited to watch *Creature Feature* on Fridays, and *Saturday Nightmares* the following evening. My imagination was gripped by the old films starring Dracula, Frankenstein, the Werewolf and the Creature from the Black Lagoon.

I had two other luxuries. On weekends my mother would let me drink hot black coffee, which I would contentedly consume into the late hours of the night while watching the television shows from the safety of our couch. During the hours when there was nothing like the *Dukes of Hazzard* to capture my attention on TV, I clung to a tattered paperback American-English dictionary that had lost its front cover. There I would recline, drinking my coffee like a young scholar and studiously working my way through the pages, taking delight each time I came to a new word I could use. I developed a special fascination for dogs, and deeply enjoyed the dictionary sketches of the various breeds under their entries.

During this time in my life I developed two boyhood friendships. And they could not have been more different from one another. One friend was named Christian Shull. Christian was intensely intelligent, dignified even at that age, and played the violin. He was actually an old acquaintance of mine from Sunday school a few years earlier. Our move to this new neighborhood brought me back into his Mormon ward. Christian's mom was devoutly Mormon, though his parents had divorced at an early age. He spent the weekdays with his mother, but at least every other weekend with his father, who was something of a free spirit (very much *not* a Latter-day Saint, or a saint of any kind, at that time). When he was with his father, Christian and I were inseparable.

One of our favorite games was playing "Rich," which involved a heavy dose of imagination for both of us. We would imagine having limitless financial resources and purchasing islands, cars, mansions, and other luxuries. In order to play Rich, all you really needed is a bathrobe because, as everyone knows, rich people wear their bathrobes all through the day, as a sign of their carefree existence. It also helps to have a glass which you can repeatedly fill with Coke, because it is common knowledge that rich people drink a beverage resembling Coke pretty much 24/7 (a notion Christian had picked up from J. R. Ewing on Dallas). We both had bathrobes, and his father had plenty of Coke on hand, so we were set.

"Okay. I'll buy another million acres of land. And I'll take the race horses too," I speak into the phone, while shaking the ice around in my glass.

Looking at Christian, I calmly hang up the phone and announce, "I've got it covered. We're gonna make a mint off this deal." Christian flashes an evil smile, while puffing on his makeshift cigar. "Time for us to order some steak and lobster," he suggests.

Our other obsession was *Star Wars*. In 1977-1978 every child who had a pulse lived in a world dominated by *Star Wars*. Attending *Star Wars* at the local movie theater was a rite of passage. I had never been to a movie before, and this film had a magical power upon the imagination. I tried on numerous occasions to levitate items through the powers of concentration, applying the principles of The Force, but it never seemed to accomplish much.

My favorite character by far was Chewbacca, whereas Christian favored Darth Vader. One Halloween he dressed up in a Vader costume which made me deeply envious. We purchased *Star Wars* cards (we both had collections numbering in the multiple hundreds), and always asked for *Star Wars* action figures and accessories on birthdays and Christmas. A book I received one Christmas, in which *Star Wars* scenes were depicted through vivid photos and pop-ups, still holds a powerful grip on my memory and affections, though it has long since gone the way of all childhood treasures.

We traded our cards and played with our action figures endlessly. Christian's collection was far superior to mine (he even had some of the space ships), but my mother had managed to buy me enough of them to keep me satisfied. The cards of course cost us money, and for that we did chores for our mothers and for a kind old lady in the neighborhood (mostly pulling weeds and yard work); but our main source of income was collecting soda cans and trading them in for cash at the local Jiffy Mart. We must have been industrious, as we always had a few dollars on hand to buy a pack of trading cards and some candy. Trash bags bulging with used cans, we would approach the clerk with our treasure, hearts aflutter at the thought of chocolate coins, licorice, and gum.

My other friend at that time was Ty Cook. He lived in the neighborhood with his father, who rarely seemed to be around. I don't remember his mother being anywhere in the picture. Ty was a very tough character, even at the age of eight. All the second and third graders at Emerson Elementary, and even some of the larger fourth graders, feared him on the playground. I spent a lot of time with Ty when Christian was not around.

Ty introduced me to the dark arts of childhood. We threw rocks at everything, but especially birds. Somehow, it was a given that song birds are the mortal enemies of boys, and must be killed on sight. Fortunately for the birds, and for our souls, our aim was poor, and we rarely gave them more than a fright.

On one occasion though, while playing at a nearby park, I thought for sure I hit a robin with a carefully placed rock. I was immediately ashamed and mortified. I rushed to the spot and looked everywhere for a sign of the poor creature, but he was nowhere to be found. I was glad not to find him, as it allowed me to imagine that he had escaped uninjured. Nobody had to tell me, for I knew deep down inside that throwing rocks at birds for amusement was morally repugnant. It is the first time I can recall being conscious of what a theologian might call "sin." Sin, I think, is whatever makes you run when God comes to investigate.

Ty introduced me to other mysteries which bit by bit took away my childish innocence. We threw rocks at cars, the windows of local homes, even other children. He showed me how to make a spear by pulling branches off of trees and sharpening them on the sidewalk. The spear was to be used both for personal protection and for hunting the neighborhood cats, which were also marked for death. The thought of killing a cat horrified me, though I never told Ty I thought that way about it. Fortunately, we never posed much of a threat to the local feline population with our crude weapons. On one occasion though he stopped by our apartment and knocked on the front screen door. I quickly ran to greet him.

"Hurry, I want to show you something cool," he urged.

I closed the screen door behind me and went with him. Arriving at a nearby driveway, I discovered that Ty and two other children had caught a small water snake and were pelting the poor thing with rocks. The pavement was spattered with blood from the crime scene. The snake slithered to and fro as it tried to escape the cruelty of the child-gods, but it was doomed, hemmed in on every side by a wrathful providence. I looked on at the spectacle with horror, helpless to intervene. I had never seen a live snake before, and couldn't understand why this harmless little creature had to die.

Ty also introduced me to porn. I was hanging around at his house one afternoon, when he told me yet again he had something "cool" to show me. He then disclosed his father's hidden stack of adult magazines. I sat with wide-eyed amazement as we giggled and thumbed our way through copies of *Playboy* and *Penthouse*. I had never seen or imagined such things before. Looking at the bodies of nude women opened the door to a world that I never knew existed. Their feminine shapes and details were astonishing to me.

For amusement we depended mostly on two sources—pocket knives and matches. I had somehow managed to convince my mother to let me carry one of my father's old pocket knives around the neighborhood, long since dulled with age, but still capable of doing some damage. We played a game with our knives in which we spread our legs apart from a standing position on the grass, while the other child would throw the knife, seeing how close he could come to your foot without impaling you and without you losing your nerve and moving. No harm ever befell us from this game, despite its potential for a trip to the Emergency Room.

But matches were another matter. We frequently lit fires around the neighborhood, burning paper in the flames and then stomping the fires out. On one hot summer's day, we were engaged in this amusing exercise in the midst of a field next to a parking lot near my home. I lit a flame amidst some branches, burned up a bit of paper, and then proceeded to stomp out the fire. But this time the fire refused to die, and quickly spread amid the dry grass and branches. The more I stomped the more the flames rebelled, as they took on a life of their own and greedily consumed their surroundings. Ty quickly made a panicked exit for home, leaving me on my own to deal with the consequences. I rushed to a nearby house and breathlessly reported that somebody had started a fire in the weeds by the parking lot. The fire department soon arrived and put out the now considerable inferno before it reached any homes or vehicles.

Suspicions, of course, focused on me from the beginning. I was certain I would be heading to prison that day. A fireman sat me down and asked if there was any chance I had caused the fire by accident. Initially I denied any and all involvement, apart from reporting the blaze of course.

"Do you know who might have started the fire then? You can tell me."

I shook my head to say "no," but I didn't get very far before my story began to crack. Thinking to deflect blame from myself, I then appealed to brute necessity. Yes, I *had* started the fire, but, "I did it to stay warm." Because, it was so cold outside . . . in the summer.

I was admonished, but I escaped criminal prosecution for my mischief. A week or so later, the firemen gave me a guided tour of their station. I had made the fireman who interrogated me promise to let me slide down the pole at the station as I had seen many times on TV, but when the opportunity came and I was escorted to the pole, I looked down at the floor far below and lost my nerve. I remember how far the ground below me seemed, and how distant the pole I would have to reach out and grab. It seemed miles away.

Apart from my friends, the other dominant image from those years is the winter. The winters are very cold in Idaho, and children need warm clothing and snow boots. My mom must have found it hard to purchase adequate winter wear, as I had to wear socks on my hands to protect them from the winter's bitter temperatures. I did have snow boots to wear, but they always seemed to have holes in the bottom from the day I got them. By the time I made it to school, the bottoms of my boots were always filled with compacted snow, and my feet wet, numb and frozen.

Around this same time I can remember being called into the school office, where various officials made a fuss about my hair. I remember one of them attempting to run a comb through my hair and noting all the dirt, knots and tangles. Apparently I was in need of a good wash and a haircut.

"Just look at this," she said as the comb stuck in my hair. "When is the last time this boy had a proper bath?"

Other matters must have been discussed as well, as I was confronted by a new earnestness at home from my mother about my breakfast. It was now imperative that I not leave for school until I had eaten a hot bowl of oatmeal, much to my chagrin. I tried my best to protest.

"Blagh. That's gross." I push away my bowl.

"Eat it, Paul" she insists. "You can't leave until you've finished."

No matter how much sugar was poured on top, I found the taste of oatmeal revolting. It still brings a sickening taste to my mouth when I think of it. Looking back, I have to wonder if social services sent someone to investigate the care I was receiving at home. I guess it was no easy thing for a tired, unemployed, single mother in her forties, plagued by handicaps and living off the mercies of government welfare, to raise a child, especially through the harsh winter months.

I was always a wanderer. During the summer I spent a great deal of time exploring the streets downtown, either alone, or with Ty or Christian (never at the same time). I would stare into shop windows, amble casually through store aisles, and sometimes accompany Christian into the local *Dungeons and Dragons* outlet where he purchased accessories for the game. I often wandered near the beautiful Snake River, which ran through the middle of town. The loud roar of the swift currents and waterfalls fascinated me, as did the serene geese waddling along the banks. Bald eagles (which someone had told me were rare in those days) could also be seen among the trees. It was a calm, peaceful and beautiful spot, the sort of place that's very difficult to grow weary of no matter how long you stay. Like heaven I imagine.

On one occasion, I walked into a restaurant near our apartment and asked if they served any free breakfasts. I guess the manager looked on me with pity, for they promptly served me up an order of bacon, eggs (over easy), and white toast soaked in butter, along with a cold glass of milk. I vividly remember sitting at the counter, my legs swinging below, and enjoying the extravagant meal. It was a pure act of kindness, which I had done nothing to secure other than walk in and ask. I made a mental note that if hungry enough, you could always walk into a local restaurant and someone was sure to feed you. A few days later I wandered into a downtown shop and tried to secure a candy bar through the same means, but was greeted only with an unfriendly rebuke.

The landlord where we lived at that time was a kind fellow. He used to bring me his used copies of *National Geographic* magazine. It was in those magazines that I saw my first photographs of wild gorillas. Gorillas had a spellbinding effect upon me. I never tired of looking at their pictures, and longed to bring home a baby gorilla as a pet. I also developed a fascination for lions and tigers. The landlord would take me with him on errands, and we would always stop at Smith's supermarket, where he would buy me a double dip chocolate ice cream cone.

On one of our trips, I asked him an important question: "If a lion and a tiger got into a fight, which one would win?"

He appeared to take the question very seriously, and admitted it was tough to decide. He leaned in favor of the judgment that the tiger would probably "whip" the lion. He once asked me to help him plant a young apple tree behind the apartment, and when it was firmly in the soil, he talked to me about how that tree would be there for years to come. If I came back and visited when I was older, I would find a large tree in that place, he assured me. I have no idea if that tree still quietly grows there as I type, but I wonder.

One other person entered our life around this time. Her name was Terry Loescher, and she lived upstairs in the same apartment building where we resided. She worked as a dishwasher at Hudson's Café, where my mother and I often went for free meals (courtesy of Ruth Hudson). I always ordered the same thing—a cheeseburger and fries, with a Coke served in a red plastic glass. The fries were thick, hot and very greasy. It was a warm and friendly environment, filled with the salt of the earth. Grizzled war veterans, local businessmen, and an assortment of other working class folks and their families dined there. A welcoming sign met the customers as soon as they entered the establishment.

"We reserve the right to refuse service to <u>anyone</u>."

I can still hear the sound of plates and dishes clanging in the kitchen in the background, and the calling up of orders by the cook ringing in my ears as I think about the place.

In any case, Terry befriended my mother, and could often be found down in our apartment where the two of them played cards and visited, sometimes sitting in chairs outside when the weather was sunny. Terry was a very rotund divorced woman, with a friendly and playful temperament, and I immediately took a liking to her. It didn't take me long to discover that she was also a good source to turn to for spending money.

"Hey Terry," I would utter with boyish charm, putting my thin arm around her shoulders. "Do you have any money? Me and Christian were gonna go to the store and get some candy."

She smiles, opens her purse, and my eyes brighten as she hands over four dollars. "Thanks!" I shout as I run out the door.

I guess Terry provided an encouragement that my mother very much needed at that time.

Moving Up in the World (1979-1981)

When fourth grade rolled around, we had moved again. This time we were in a better situation, as Terry and my mother pooled their resources to rent a modest home on the southern end of town, only a block from the Hawthorne Elementary School. It was a yellow two-bedroom house with a large tree out front with a built-in tree house, where I could store peanut butter and other treasures. Somehow we procured a washer and dryer, saving us the trips back and forth to the laundromat. And for the first time in my memory I had my own bedroom rather than sleeping in cots in the kitchen area as in the previous apartments.

It was during this period that a new consciousness of the opposite sex first began to manifest itself. I befriended a girl named Pam Woolf and often walked her home from school. One day during recess she told me she had something to say to me and directed me to sit down with her on the grass. There we sat facing each other, our legs crossed and our arms resting along the front of our knees. Then, with her girlish finger, she silently wrote three words, suspending them in the air with some magical feminine power and directed me to read them aloud.

I . . . Love . . . You.

I clumsily reciprocated her actions, though with less dramatic flair. And so it all began.

Her presence calmed me. She seemed to let me do most of the talking as we walked along after school, looking at me with a comforting expression somewhere between amusement and affection. From time to time I would go over to her house, which was only a few blocks from where I lived. It was a spacious two-story house with a big front porch, the sort you would sit on in the early evenings of the summer, rocking in the porch chair with a glass of Coke in your hand. Serenely one might watch cars drive by and listen to the crickets whisper their secrets to the trees. We would either eat snacks in her kitchen or listen to records in her bedroom, which was lushly decorated with posters suited to the tastes of little girls and a plethora of stuffed animals.

Her mother always treated me with kindness and appeared to be satisfied with her daughter's choice of first childhood love. Somehow I expected Pam's family not to receive me with much enthusiasm. I was aware without needing to be told that I was poor, and they were not. I did not really belong in their world, and eventually would need to find my way back to my own realm. But Pam's mother totally disarmed me with her kindness and shattered my assumptions. Pam and her mother were happy to allow me to sit and rest by the warmth of their fireside for the time being.

Circumstances changed as I moved to a different neighborhood in my sixth grade year, and of course we drifted apart. But Pam's mother was still observant enough a few years later to see the notice of my mother's death in the newspaper, and they signed the consolation book at the funeral home.

I remember next to nothing about my fourth grade teacher, but in the fifth grade I was in Mr. Craig's class. He was a young teacher, with glasses and black hair, probably late twenties at the time, very tall, with an excellent sense of humor that related well to children.

The whole class adored him. Mr. Craig seemed to take a special interest in me. He spoke to me in a fatherly way that bolstered my self-esteem. That year we participated in the Presidential Physical Fitness Program. All of us went through the routine of the testing, which involved doing pull-ups, sit-ups and various other activities, including timed running. Mr. Craig told me I had talent. So, while most of the children probably went through the paces with the intent of qualifying for the national award, including a certificate endorsed with the signature of President Ronald Reagan, I toiled to secure the admiration of Mr. Craig.

The long distance running component of the exam was a disappointing experience for me. I ran fast, at a pace that put me in position to finish with the fastest time in the fifth grade class. But I became confused in the final stretch and somehow misjudged the location of the finish line. To my dismay, I had stopped about fifty feet short of the line. Mr. Craig shouted for me to keep running to a point ahead of me, but by the time I had recovered my senses and once again taken flight, I had missed the opportunity for first place. All boys seem to have the desire to gain the approval of a man, and for me, in the fifth grade, that man was Mr. Craig.

Sometimes during class I would study him, like a National Geographic naturalist might observe a lion on the Serengeti Plain. Mr. Craig often sat at his desk, reading the newspaper with a bottle of Coke in his hand (those nostalgic old glass bottles), his feet perched on the desktop like a security guard serving his shift while we worked on some assignment. Sometimes he would look up and notice me gazing at him, and he would simply wink at me, with a twitch of a smile, then return to his reading. One wink, one twitch of a smile from Mr. Craig gripped my heart in ways that defy description.

I often wonder how my psyche has been shaped by the lack of such winks at home while growing up. My mother was simply incapable of offering me a fatherly wink. I might as well have asked her to flap her arms and fly through the air. Mothers cannot sit perched like security guards while reading the newspaper, and tantalize the hearts of boys. Every day, boys wake up to a world full of possibility. They may be rewarded by a wink, a smile, a ruffling of the hair, or some other god-like outpouring of grace from their fathers. That was never the world to which I awoke, and it never will be.

I did not find it an easy thing to get up in the mornings, especially in the winter. In the morning before school I had a ritual which I meticulously followed, with the precision of a priest performing the Eucharist. I would emerge from my bedroom in my bathrobe with my eyes closed, ignoring my mother and Terry, and walk over to the heating vent in the dining area. There I would lie down on the floor and allow my wiry body to soak up the delicious warmth of the blowing air. I emerged from a winter den every morning encrusted with frost and ice, until God's warm breath thawed me, pulling me into the delights of a new spring day.

Nights were unpleasant times for me, broken by constant nightmares and imaginings of a dark presence visiting my bedroom. He would come down the hall and stand at the doorway. Silently, he would stare at me on the bed, blocking the only route of access to my mother in the adjacent room. I would stare back for awhile, trying to face my fear, until finally I would scream for my mother to bring me a glass of water. Hearing her steps coming down the hallway, he would always flee.

I continued to visit Christian in those days, in his now distant neighborhood. Ty had passed out of my sphere of contact, to march alone into whatever less-than-hopeful future fate had in store for him.

In the summer prior to my fourth grade year, Christian was assigned to a summer school program held at Hawthorne Elementary, which afforded me convenient opportunities to visit him.

At set times during the day, lunch and recess, I would walk over to the school and meet him by the fence. There through the chain link we would talk, like a lonely wife visiting a hardened prisoner. I wonder what we talked about during those hot summer days. My timed visits with Christian were important to me, and I would never miss them if it was within my childish powers. Perhaps Christian represented a link to my past, an anchor in the waters of my life, which always seemed to be taking me in new and unexpected directions.

Another childhood character that stands out to me from this period was Michael Ng. He was a friend from Hawthorne Elementary. He was small and extremely thin, even compared to me. His parents had immigrated to America from China some time before he was born. They owned and operated a Chinese restaurant downtown and also managed the small apartment building in which they lived. Visiting Michael in his home was like exploring an exotic country. A stern land, in which people spoke to one another in loud and serious tones, usually in a foreign tongue that barked ominously throughout the building. I can never recall a light-hearted moment when being there. Before entering the apartment, it was absolutely imperative that one first remove his shoes.

Their home smelled odd to me, too, though I could never quite identify the source of the strange odor. The smells that greeted me in the doorway told me to tread softly, for I did not belong there. Whenever I visited, I would timidly knock and wait for one of Michael's parents to answer. When one or the other came to the door, I was always greeted with a suspicious stare, mixed with mild annoyance, as though this were the first time I had ever appeared on their property, and they were unsure of my true identity.

With nervous ten-year-old eyes darting in every direction, I would sheepishly ask if Michael was home, with the sort of tone in my voice a teenager might use while purchasing condoms. Then I would wait at the doorway until he came out, and we would quickly make our escape while the opportunity permitted safe passage. Occasionally we would sneak down into the basement where his bedroom was, and close the door to escape into a world of comic book fantasy.

The one passion Michael and I shared was comic books. Marvel comic books, that is. We showed no interest in the DC series. That meant characters such as Spider Man, the Incredible Hulk, and the Fantastic Four, not Bat Man, Super Man or other such banalities. We had comic book collections numbering in the hundreds. I shudder to think what our collections would be worth today. We usually purchased our comics second-hand from a local teenage dealer who readily accepted the spare change on our weekly visits. Comic book heroes and their exploits created an alternative universe for the two of us, where Michael could escape his yelling parents and the beatings of his older brother Frank. As I accompanied the heroes on their journeys, I too could escape from my world, a world that was full of discontent and angst and boredom, the source of which continued to elude me.

My images of my mother from that period are not very positive. She comes into my consciousness as a nagging, restraining figure, struggling to hold down my natural boyish impulses. She sets up boundaries at every turn. *Don't go too far. Don't play like that. Don't hand around with him. Don't stay out too long.* She discouraged me from involvement in school sports, and was constantly worried about me getting injured. She was unable to be something that I needed. There was a longing within my ten-year-old heart that no mother could satisfy. And I resented her for that, though she never returned my hostility.

I would periodically run away in the summer evenings, knowing that it terrified her, and hide out near the river or along the railroad tracks until I lost my nerve long after dark and returned home. I was told once, when my habit of running away was the topic of conversation, that this pattern of behavior first started when I was about 6 years old. I was discovered by some Good Samaritan wandering the aisles of a downtown supermarket called the Savings Center. When asked what I was doing, I straightforwardly answered, "I'm looking for my daddy."

Michael Ng was an artist with apparent potential, who obsessively drew sketches of Spider Man. His unwavering ambition was to go to art school and become a comic book artist when he grew up. I had no clear vocational direction at that age, though I toyed with the idea of living off the land as a mountain man. I envisioned finishing school, saying goodbye to my crying mother, and walking up into the mountains, where I would quickly focus on the task of building a winter shelter, picking wild berries, and hunting game for food. I guess I must have read about mountain men somewhere, or seen such characters on the TV. Strangely enough, the life of a mountain man holds no appeal to me now.

One noteworthy experience stands out in this period of time. During the summer of 1980, after finishing fourth grade, my mother and Terry purchased us tickets for a trip to Mexico. I had never traveled much and was extremely excited at the prospect of visiting far away places.

We traveled on a Greyhound bus down through Salt Lake City, over to Las Vegas, down to Hollywood and Disneyland, and then south to Tijuana. Then we retraced our path back to Idaho Falls. Often I sat near the front of the bus and peppered the poor driver with constant questions. Early in the first leg of the trip he made the fatal mistake of claiming to have been an acquaintance of John Wayne, and from that point on I was a moth banging into the lamp in the driver's seat. I was convinced he knew all the mysteries of Hollywood and the movie stars. When driving through the Salt Lake City area I repeatedly asked him to signal when we were approaching the neighborhood where the movie stars lived. Finally, with an exasperated wave of his left arm toward some lights to the east of the freeway, he said, "Up in those hills there." It was night, and I stared through the darkness toward the distant homes with awe, while some families watched TV and others put their children to bed, oblivious to my piercing gaze.

I only have vague memories of the trip for the most part. We stayed at a hotel in Las Vegas. It had a swimming pool, which fascinated me, though I never dared enter the water. We visited various casinos and locations along the strip. I saw large stone lions staring at me, amidst a bewildering array of cars, lights and tourists. I was sure I would see somebody famous from the movies, though my hope never materialized. At one point I stood for awhile on the balcony of our hotel room, staring for a long time at a white limousine parked down below. I was sure that only movie stars rode in limousines, but no such people emerged, and the limousine driver never seemed aware of my presence.

During the bus drive I mostly occupied myself with the Marvel comic books I brought along, and my Star Wars action figures, when I was not gazing out the window at the lonely sagebrush in the desert. Hollywood and Disneyland are a blur in my memory. Hot weather and traffic. But I was disappointed at Disneyland when my requests for autographs from Mickey Mouse and other characters were consistently refused. I literally believed that the costumed figures greeting me in the amusement park *were* the actual characters I had seen on TV in cartoon form. After all, they lived at Disneyland, didn't they? In any event, a world in which Goofy refused to give his autograph to a little boy is not what I expected to encounter in that fantasyland.

So we journeyed down, further south. Tijuana was hellish—hot, crowded and poor—and after collecting some memorabilia, including a sheepskin cowboy vest for me, we didn't stay long. The height of the bus kept the small children on the street below from looking directly into the windows at us at stops and traffic lights, which is probably why I was largely unconscious of their big, dark eyes and earnest, dirty faces. How many of them, in the summer of 1980, looked up at me in the window with my cowboy vest, and wondered what it would be like to be touring the southwest on a Greyhound bus? And where are they now I wonder? I guess I'll never know.

Keith (1981)

After my fifth grade year, in the summer of 1981, we moved from the yellow house to a different part of town. My mother, Terry and I happily settled into a nice suburban neighborhood on the east side of town, where we rented a duplex home. This place was nicer than the one before, and not only did I have my own room, but a large basement as well. I had never lived in a home with a basement before. I loved this new neighborhood. The yards were well kept, with healthy green grass and idyllic fences at every turn.

A funny thing happened that summer. For some reason, it was determined that I should spend some time living with my cousins Keith and Sandy Birch out in Howe, Idaho. Sandy was the daughter of Aunt Bonnie, my mother's sister with whom I had lived for a time as a toddler. Keith was a ranch worker, mechanic and local hand of various trades. They lived in a rented trailer on some farm land belonging to his employer. The idea was presented to me as a chance to be in the outdoors for a summer, to breathe clean air and experience the wholesome routines of country living. I got the impression that while my mother had gone along with the idea, the suggestion had originated from elsewhere. So, one afternoon early in the summer, Keith and Sandy, three children in tow, pulled up in front of our duplex to pick me up.

I was in awe of Keith from the first moment I saw him. He was a tall, thin, muscular man, about 30 years old at the time. He wore tight, faded jeans and a cap with the name of some trucking company on it. He had a mustache and smelled of beer and sweat. He kept his hair cut short most of the time; when it grew out you could tell it was already thinning. When his hair was combed to the side, slicked back with water, he looked just like the cowboys you see in old western photos from the 19th century. He seemed to belong still to a world that was fading fast away.

There they were in our living room, Keith and Sandy, and the children, Cory, Lance and Tasha, ages seven, four and two. The children sat there without a word, while their parents exchanged pleasantries with my mother, assuring her that a summer on a farm, and a bit of hard work would be good for my character.

"Oh he'll love it, Leona," Sandy coos, as she adjusts her antsy toddler on her lap. "A little hard work will do this boy some good. Right Paul?"

She looks at me. I look at my mother. Then I shrug my shoulders and nod a compulsory yes. I was uneasy about this adventure, but willing to go along, knowing at least that it would take me to places I had yet to see and experience. So after some time, I hugged Terry and my mother and climbed into the crowded, sun-bathed seat of their old, tan-colored, "half-ton" Chevy pickup truck.

I studied the old radio, and the surroundings of my new environment. I saw the discarded carcasses of Pepsi, beer, and cigarettes. Behind me was a gun rack with two rifles, which immediately held my interest. Keith started the ignition, a cigarette dangling from his mouth. The engine was loud and rumbled menacingly in a way I was not used to,

31

but I found myself liking it. He pushed the stick shift into gear in a masculine and confident sort of way, and soon we were on the freeway, headed out of town, up through the sagebrush plains of the Upper Snake River Valley, then west toward Mud Lake and the small farming community of Howe about an hour and a half away.

With a twinkle in his eye, Keith told me on the way there that Howe received its name from the question that always occurred to people whenever they arrived there.

"*How* in the hell does anyone live out here?"

If I hoped to experience some semblance of what a normal family life was like, with a father, mother and siblings, I was in for a disappointment. Almost from the beginning, Sandy made it clear that she despised me, and saw the purpose of this visit to be that of reforming my dangerous and delinquent behavior.

She was a dumpy woman in her twenties, always dressed in thin, shabby clothes, with long black hair hanging down her back. She had a bitter way about her, a bit of poison lurking beneath her frequent laughter. I was startled to discover at some point later on when looking at some photos that she had been quite pretty as a teenager, skinny, in bell bottom jeans, with that long black hair parted straight down the middle. How did she get from there to this? Sandy had been married once before; only Tasha was fathered by Keith.

Some years later, when my life had taken a very different turn, I was riding in a pickup with Keith in the winter, as we made our way to a snowmobiling spot near Bone, Idaho. Keith offered a friendly wave to a man passing by us in his own truck. He then turned to Uncle Norman and said, "Just waved at your former son-in-law, Norman." Keith proceeded to inform me that the last time he had seen that "son-of-a-bitch," he had warned him that if he ever showed up around Sandy and the kids again, "I'd kill him." I looked out my window at the snowy countryside passing by, my heart racing.

During my stay that summer, Keith alternated from a winsome father figure to a punishing bully, testing the thickness of my skin with his fist and the thickness of my psyche with the sharp bite of his words, which chipped away at my boyish self-image like a drill sergeant breaking in new recruits. I never knew which Keith I would encounter at any given moment. He seemed to delight in showing kindness and cruelty, both when I would least expect it. Early on I knew better than to ever talk back to him, as I once watched him walk out of his bedroom and knock 7-year old Cory off his feet with an open-handed slap on the side of his head, having overheard him sassing Sandy.

Keith was such an intriguing figure, intelligent, a jack-of-all-trades, skilled at mechanics, learned in agriculture and widely read in a way one would not expect of a farm worker. He knew all about trucks, nature, pocketknives, rifles, the arts of hunting and fishing and wildlife. He loved dogs, the outdoors, and working in the open field. He was a Vietnam vet, and had helped with the training of military dogs. He could lecture on the respective merits of Dobermans, German Shepherds, and Airedales as attack dogs.

Keith smoked cigarettes in a manly sort of way that inspired my boyish affection. He drank Pepsi and Budweiser with a manner that comes only to those who work hard outside for a living. He wore cowboy boots and thin polyester cowboy shirts. His voice sounded like the father every boy dreams of having.

In his younger days he had spent some time in the ominous youth detention facility up at St. Anthony. He told me lots of stories about his teenage exploits, mostly evil, occasionally winsome, always vulgar. He spent most of his time in those days fighting other boys, and torturing neighborhood cats in unspeakable ways.

Keith, at the end of the day, was a cruel and vicious man. I would find out that he took delight in causing terror in the weak, which definitely included me. One of his favorite forms of amusement turned out to be punching my shoulder with some force when I would least expect it.

Smack.

The hardened knuckles of a man, colliding with the thin shoulder of a nervous boy.

He would then stare at me, dragging on his cigarette, to determine whether I would cry. When I did cry, he would always apologize, holding me in a fatherly way, rubbing my shoulder to offer comfort. If I continued to sob, he would tickle me until I stopped. It always worked.

For an animal lover, which he actually did seem to be at certain times, he could be shockingly callous to the suffering of his pets. He was Dr. Jekyll and Mr. Hyde where both people and animals were concerned. One of my enduring images from that summer is their small white cat, which wandered around inside the trailer, and lay on the lawn outside, coughing constantly. She had a glazed and fevered look in her eyes, and a horrible wound festering on her neck, as small children carried her around like a toy in some insane world. She had swallowed some fish bones that had failed to make it down all the way and had become lodged in her throat, working their way through her flesh over time until they now protruded in a bloody, infected wound.

Taking the cat to a vet was out of the question for folks like Keith and Sandy. Animals are there to add some touch on the scenery, until they die. It's nothing to get overly anxious about when the cat disappears or the dog gets sick. What one would expect would be a merciful .22 bullet in the head of this creature, but it turns out Keith was keeping the cat alive so she could continue to nurse her kittens. What must the world have seemed like to that cat, as her kittens struggled for position beneath her, surrounded by the sounds of children's voices, footsteps on trailer floor, and distant birds outdoors?

Years later I would ask him whatever became of the cat.

"She died," Keith told me with a measured stare as he calmly smoked.

"How?" I asked.

"Lead poisoning," came his witty reply, as he blew the last drag of smoke toward me and put out a cigarette.

That summer I spent many hot days weeding their large outdoor garden, where they grew vegetables, and began to wonder if the true purpose of my summer adventure centered on this daunting task. When I became too weary from the blazing sun, and the depth of those immense weeds beneath the soil, I would sneak over to the cheap wooden steps and creep up to the front door of the trailer, from which I would watch episodes of *General Hospital* and other soap operas from behind Sandy's lazy chair.

I was fascinated by the epic love story of Luke and Laura that was going on that summer, and the other threads of plot that captivated my attention. How long will Laura make Luke wait? How long will the patience of his love endure?

A few memories stay with me from those weeks of rustic living, besides the poor family cat. Once I was playing with some children on a farm nearby, and we found a couple of local kids excitedly banging on the wall of a barn. The children had discovered that a nest of mice lived within the barn wall. Eventually a tiny baby mouse, blood emitting from its nose, dropped out of the wall where its mother had hidden it, and landed on the dirt below. Everyone studied its lifeless little corpse with interest. The scene haunts me to this day.

On another occasion that summer we were visiting with a local family in Howe. This family raised pigs, and at some point I was told that one of the piglets was deathly ill and would probably not live much longer. I was asked if I would like to hold the piglet while it was still alive. I did, and asked if I could keep the creature in my lap while the families visited and played cards.

And so there I sat through the evening, holding this baby pig, the size of a puppy, in my lap on a blanket. It moved occasionally, its body warm, its ears laid back, as I held it close and offered it comfort. I was helpless to keep this infant alive, helpless to offer any practical assistance. As with the little mouse, all I could do is stand by and watch it die. I held it close to my chest, and gently stroked its little neck and head until its labored breathing grew still. After awhile I handed the corpse back to the family. Though we only met for a brief time, I formed a bond with that helpless animal that I will never forget, and I like to believe it was conscious of my love, and my hurt, as it quietly left this world. It died in the arms of someone who cared.

The Birch family had a dog named Rowdy. Rowdy was part Doberman Pinscher, part Blue Heeler, and tough as nails. He was tolerant of the family children, but gave me vibes that warned me that I had best leave him alone. Keith seldom fed Rowdy much beyond some table scraps now and then. So Rowdy hunted the fields around their trailer for mice and rabbits that he would bring home, and he seemed to subsist fairly well under such half-domesticated conditions.

One of Keith's favorite pastimes was to hunt jackrabbits by spotlight at night from his pickup, wounding them with his .22 and then allowing Rowdy to finish them off, filling the moonlit sky with their blood-curdling squeals. They sounded like babies screaming for their mothers. Months later, while engaged in this haunting "sport," Keith overturned his pickup and crushed Rowdy to death underneath the bed of the truck.

Keith described this experience to me at my Aunt Bonnie and Uncle Norman's trailer years later.

"It's hard to describe the feelings I had for Rowdy," he said.

"What do you mean?" I asked.

Keith looked me in the eyes and said, "I would have given my life for that dog."

He meant it. He spoke it like one might imagine a soldier speaking of his war buddies on the battle field. That is the way Keith looked at life at the end of the day. He could never look at the world as anything but a war, filled with pain and brutality, punctuated by rare moments of simple goodness, which derive their value from the darkness of their surroundings.

Keith and Rowdy faced the world together, a world full of memories of atrocities both committed and endured. Each day a battle to maintain some sense of meaning, while surrounded by the bleakness of reality in a rural wasteland. Rented trailers, meager paychecks, repaired pickup trucks, irrigation ditches, grease, mud and grime—these were the foes with which Keith and Rowdy grappled on the front lines of Howe, Idaho. When that pickup crushed the life out of Rowdy, it must have crushed half the life out of Keith as well.

Almost from the beginning of that summer, Keith had inspired me with the hope of a puppy from a litter sired by Rowdy. The puppies would be three-quarters Blue Heeler and one-quarter Doberman from a breeding of Rowdy and a local Heeler bitch.

I dreamed of that puppy all through the summer, imagined playing with it, what it would smell like, and the feel of it in my arms. I could see myself on the trip home, with this puppy sleeping contentedly on my lap while I gazed out the window at the passing scenery. I thought through the characteristics such a mixed breeding would likely produce, and thus was able to envision in some detail the personality and appearance of my new dog once he was full grown. Heaven help any intruder who would be foolish enough to try and break into our house!

But alas, the summer came and went. Keith told me that other people had already claimed all the puppies, but that maybe I could get one from the next batch.

From time to time, Keith took his boys and me fishing with him, and on family camping trips in the area. At nights we would roast hot dogs and marshmallows on an open fire beneath the stars. Sometimes Keith would let me climb into the hot cab of his pickup and come with him to his work, where he would walk through the open fields in his rubber boots, carrying his shovel over his shoulder like a soldier's rifle, while changing sprinkler pipes and handling the irrigation systems.

I was amazed at how long his legs were, and how easily and gracefully he moved along while he worked. As we traveled from site to site, he would keep me spellbound with stories of deer hunting, the merits of various dog breeds, and other bits and pieces of manly insights about women, work and wildlife. He pointed me toward the mountains, and told me of the elk and black bear that roamed the distant forests, which tantalized my imagination as my eyes surveyed the horizon. But I was very thankful when the summer finally passed, and the time came to return to Idaho Falls, the comforts of our duplex, and the security of my mother's presence.

Sixth Grade (1981-1982)

The school I attended for sixth grade, Linden Park Elementary, was only a couple of blocks from my house, and I found it surprisingly easy to settle in with the other children there. I had plenty of friends to play with, though none of them made much of a lasting impression on my memory. There was one exception though. I often played with an extremely intelligent but conspicuously foul-mouthed boy named Brian. He was built like a little scarecrow and had bright red hair and freckles. Brian had a tendency to get picked on a lot.

We often spent our time making crude bombs behind his backyard. We would fill beer, wine and soda bottles with cologne and other fuels, plug the opening with a rag, set the rag on fire, and then toss the thing to watch it explode. Brian sticks in my memory because even at 11 years of age, he was an avowed atheist, something I had never encountered before. He insisted that he believed in *science*, not "fucking fairy tales" like God. I had no real arguments to present to him to prove the existence of the Deity, but I still felt pretty sure there was a God somehow.

We agreed to disagree, and continued our bomb-making exploits with very little conflict.

At some point however, we devised a bizarre plan to take over the world. Why we had the desire to do something like that is still unclear to me. To do so, we would need to build a nuclear bomb. We could get the Russians to help us with that end of things. However, before using such a weapon, it would first need to be tested out in the desert. This is where our capacity for cooperation in the pursuit of evil began to fall apart.

I asked Brian a simple question which I was sure he had not considered. If we exploded such a bomb out in the desert, what would become of the coyotes, jackrabbits and other little animals that inhabited those places? How would we be able to make sure that no harm came to them? His loud response was a bit surprising to me, though the rhetorical flair with which he expressed it was not.

"Who gives a fuck about the fucking animals?" he said, looking at me with a disgusted expression, as though I had completely taken leave of my senses.

I insisted then that in good conscience, I would not be able to support such a scheme. Soon after our friendship fizzled.

Sixth grade would prove to be a great year for me. For the first time in my life, I began to get good grades, and received nearly all A's, with only a couple B's. Up to this point, my grades had been a mixture of C's and D's, with an occasional B. It was a dramatic turnaround, which my mother proudly took note of.

My sixth grade teacher was a wonderful, grey-haired woman named Mrs. Williams. She was stern but fair, a no-nonsense disciplinarian of the old school, who cared deeply about her students. She exposed me to a rich variety of literature. At her prompting I began to read a host of classics in young adult literature like, *The Lion, the Witch and the Wardrobe, Where the Red Fern Grows, Summer of the Monkeys, A Swiftly*

Tilting Planet, A Wind in the Door, Big Red, Irish Red, Outlaw Red, Desert Dog, Lion Hound, The Call of the Wild, White Fang, Yellow Eyes and *Broken Fang* among others. I never realized how much I could love reading things besides comic books until she guided me along the path of literary discovery.

Providence really seemed to be smiling on us that year. My memories are mostly warm and colorful. Sitting on the front porch during hot weather, while chatting with neighbors; being sent by mom and Terry on errands to the local convenience store to buy ice cream and sodas. I even got involved with the Boy Scouts, who met at one of the local Mormon wards. No longer did I throw rocks at cars and birds, nor did I pretend to hunt cats with childhood thugs. Popular at school, secure at home, confident in the knowledge that life was finally taking a turn for the better in our little family. I was, for the first time I can really recall up to that point, content.

I think my mother was pretty content as well, and my memories of her are no longer of a nagging figure, but of a nurturing homebody, greeting me on my return from school and asking me about the adventures of the day. I think she was as happy then as she had ever been in her 47 years.

She and Terry played the card game "Canasta" constantly, often late into the night, the kitchen full of smoke from Terry's cigarettes, like the Holy of Holies in the Jewish Temple. I can still see my mother sitting in our living room chair, pursuing her simple pleasures throughout the day. She loved to do crossword puzzles and read the latest gossip in *TV Guide* and the *National Inquirer*. Her morning routine always started with "Good Morning America" on the TV as I got ready for school.

Her ragged appearance is still vivid to me. She was a small woman, with short dark hair, never properly cared for. She rarely visited a hair stylist, and it was clear that her dental care was in a state of neglect. Her drab wardrobe was purchased second-hand from local charity shops.

She was only married to my father for a few short years, and much of that time saw them separated by his illness. So what did she have to dress up for really?

Her mannerisms were quiet and reflective. She often sat with her right palm resting under her chin, her fingers running up the length of her jaw as she read or watched TV. Her deformed left hand was usually resting at her side underneath her leg, or nestled, hiding, beneath her right armpit as she whittled away the hours in our quiet home.

She loved to talk on the phone with friends and distant relatives, an assorted variety of poor, elderly and unfortunate women scattered around the area. One of her closest friends was an old lady named "Othello" who lived in a modest little country house in Roberts. Sometimes mom would limp across town to visit someone or another, and bring me along, for company I suppose. I can still see myself a step or so behind her, like a black bear cub following a wounded sow through the woods, reluctant and frustrated at such a waste of my valuable time.

My mother was intelligent, in a tentative and uneducated sort of way. I am sure that she had an active, introspective way of looking at life and the world around her. She rarely spoke out or had occasion to discuss the various and assorted issues that occupy the minds of intellectuals. I never heard her declare her perspectives on politics, the economy, abortion and birth control, euthanasia, the environment, the merits of space exploration, theology, philosophy, ancient history or foreign cultures. Life's experiences did not provide her the confidence to formulate dogmatic stances or pontificate from established platforms.

But as I recall her in my mind's eye, I am sure now she watched the world with a measured stare, seasoned by constant suffering and limitations at every turn, quietly taking in the world's issues and mysteries, while pondering many things silently. She always wanted to return to high school and earn her diploma; it seems to have been an unfulfilled ambition of hers. She wanted to at least make some small mark on the world, to be forever memorialized as a graduate of some specific year at Rigby High School or wherever she would have finished.

Her roommate Terry continued to live with us, and also seemed as happy as I could ever remember her being. Terry had long brown hair and was much taller and heavier than my mother. And she was a chain smoker.

I love the smell of tobacco, the cadence of the motions involved in smoking. There is something about the mannerisms and rhythms created by smoking which calms the soul, invites contemplation, makes the world seem a little less hostile. Like walking in the woods, smoking enacts a ritual which we engage in for no higher end than the act itself. It serves no purpose outside itself, and such actions always convey the deepest meaning.

Not only does smoking serve no higher purpose, it involves a sacrifice, as the action itself takes a toll upon the body. We give something of ourselves, we lose and offer up ourselves in order to receive something back of greater value. Smoking cigarettes, like falling in love, heals the broken spirit, though not without a cost.

Better to live and smoke, than not to smoke at all? I've heard worse life mottos.

Terry the smoker loved to laugh, whether at the antics of others or her own exploits. She adored Neil Diamond and the movie *The Jazz Singer*, which we enjoyed watching together. She played the soundtrack from that movie at our house almost daily. She was more adept than my mother at relating to my adolescent ways. She talked to me about the world and what it was like to live in far away places, like Spokane where she lived with her husband in a former life. She talked to me about "the birds and the bees," and how one day I would fall in love and marry and raise a family of my own. She was able to relax in a way that life had not conditioned my mother to do, and took a "boys will be boys" sort of attitude to most problems. Together, they seemed to be a pretty good team.

From time to time as I have told my story, people have asked about the nature of the relationship between Terry and my mother. Were they just friends and roommates, or were they "partners"? Ultimately, I have no way of knowing for sure what took place in their private life, but all I can say is, if there was anything romantic going on, they kept it well-hidden from me. They never held hands, cuddled, kissed or spoke in a romantic way in my presence, and they slept in separate beds. Terry used to speak fondly of her ex-husband and the life she had shared with him. I always got the sense that he had broken her heart. So I have to assume that they were just good friends who helped each other with finances and the struggles of daily life.

MacTavish of Idaho, C.D. (1982)

For as long as I can remember I have loved dogs. Throughout my childhood I pestered my mother for a dog from time to time, but the rental conditions of our apartments always prevented it. That summer with Keith and Sandy, which I spent fantasizing about the puppy from Rowdy's litter I never received, poured fuel on the fire of my lust. When I returned at the end of the summer the topic of a puppy was frequently raised at our kitchen table.

Two other experiences fostered a longing within me to bring home a canine companion. During show and tell in sixth grade, a girl brought in her new Scottish Terrier puppy for the class to see. I was enamored with the energy and life that coursed through its little, black body as it wriggled in her arms. My wish for a dog was also nurtured by something I noticed, not long after we moved into the duplex. As you walked out our back door you would see a medium-sized, grassy yard, bordered by a wooden fence separating us from the houses behind us, and garages on either side of the lawn. One day while playing out there, I noticed that I could look behind the garage on the right through a gap into the adjacent yard on the other side. I peeked back there and saw a large black and tan dog, with wiry hair, standing in the yard. From the dog books I had been checking out of the public library since returning from summer break, I recognized the breed.

It was an Airedale Terrier. I was spellbound, and could easily stand at the back of the garage for the better part of an hour, lurking into the yard behind us at that beautiful dog. He was a seemingly perfect specimen of the breed, and appeared to spend most of his time patrolling the boundaries of his domestic territory, barking now and then at noises that captured his attention. Whenever he would come near my end of the yard my heart would pound with excitement. Sometimes he simply lay in the shade next to the house, casually observant of his surroundings. If he would walk out of my vision I would strain my neck into grotesque contortions to keep him in my line of sight. I was in love.

With increasing intensity over the course of that year, I began to pore over every piece of literature I could get my hands on that dealt with dog breeds. My mind was starving for knowledge, and quickly began to build up a stockpile of data about the American Kennel Club, and all the different breeds and varieties of dogs that the AKC categorized into various groups.

I read about sporting dogs, which were used for pointing, flushing and retrieving birds; hounds, which trailed game animals by scent; working dogs, which served human purposes in guarding sheep, protecting property and other tasks; terriers, who were sent in to take on varmints in close combat; toy dogs, who were developed to amuse people of leisure; and non-sporting dogs, which included all the breeds that did not fit in the other categories. If asked, I could tell you the history, country of origin, original purpose and physical features of nearly any recognized breed.

The more I studied, the more I longed for a canine friend. I had a porcelain Bulldog in my room that I attached a leash to and animated in my imagination, along with an assortment of tattered, stuffed dogs that I walked, fed and talked to constantly. In the evenings, I would read the puppies-for-sale ads in the *Post Register*, each ad causing me to pause and play out a new fantasy in my mind.

Whenever I brought up the topic to my mother, she always told me that the landlord would never let us have a dog, so there was no point in asking about it. I sensed less resistance than in the past though, and her weakening resolve raised my hopes. Eventually, Terry must have got tired of my constant pleading, and took pity on me. She came home one afternoon, hot and sweaty from a long walk. I was sitting on the front porch, watching her ponderously make her way towards me.

She looked at me sitting there and said, "I've got some good news for you."

"What?" I blurted, suddenly alert in anticipation of her announcement.

"Well," Terry began, sitting down next to me on the step. "I just came from talking with our landlord. And he said, if we guarantee him that we will make sure no damage is done to the property, that it's okay with him if you get a small dog."

I could scarcely believe what I was hearing! What I had known to this point only as a fantasy was actually becoming a reality! Within the next few days some arrangements were made by between Terry, my mom, and Ruth Hudson, and upon coming home from school one afternoon, I was told that a purebred puppy had been purchased for me. He was a 10-week old Miniature Schnauzer, bought from a local (backyard) breeder for $150 (nearly a month's rent for us back then).

I can vividly remember the magical evening the puppy was dropped off at our home. I stood in a daze at the door as the breeder entered and handed me a soft, gray bundle of wriggling flesh and fur. I set him down on the carpet and, as though in a drug-induced haze, followed him around from room to room while he sniffed and explored his new surroundings. The breeder explained to me some basic facts about feeding and caring for my new puppy and how to go about registering him with the American Kennel Club.

Later that evening, Ruth Hudson came over to see him. Together, sitting at the kitchen table, we worked on naming him. At some point, Ruth made the suggestion that he be called "MacTavish of Idaho" in his registration papers, and his nickname could be "Mac."

Originally, the plan was for Mac to sleep in a cardboard box until he was housebroken, but that didn't last for long, and within the week he was sleeping with me in the bed. His warm little body snuggled under the covers with me through the night or on top of the bed between my knees, his tiny chin resting on my leg. As his body grew, so did our bond. He studied me with warm brown eyes as I sat with him during the day, talking to him and scratching behind his ears. I stroked his neck in the dark hours. From that first night, his guileless heart clung on to me. Together, man and beast, we would face whatever challenges the world might throw at us.

Getting Mac brought me into contact with other people, who soon became central figures in my life. While walking Mac around the block one day, I met the owner of the Airedale. His name was Richard Moore. He worked at the nuclear power plant out in the desert northwest of Idaho Falls. He had been a fighter pilot during World War II and had shot down many planes. He was slight of build, of medium height for a man, with thin white hair and a protruding nose that was bulb-shaped at the end. I found out over time that he was of Native American ancestry, and had been raised in California in the early 20th century, before it had been spoiled by the growth in population. His parents had co-existed with the yet-to-be extirpated California grizzly.

Mr. Moore lived with his wife Betty. I quickly formed an attachment to him and would walk Mac around the block simply to stop by his duplex. I would stand there at the gate of his chain link fence, admiring his Airedale, Brandy, until he would notice me standing out there and casually wander outside, as though he intended to visit his back yard anyway. There we would talk, as he paused to comb his white hair, or work with Brandy on the grooming table, plucking and trimming to perfection.

Richard Moore was a lover of nature and the outdoors. As a younger man he had been an avid deer hunter and had strict ethics about the way hunters were to conduct themselves. Though he was happy to discuss rifle calibers and hunting tactics, I soon discovered he had little time for most actual hunters, viewing them as insufficiently spiritual in their contacts with nature.

Mostly we just talked about dogs. We stood on either side of his fence for long periods of time, discussing the merits of various breeds. Like me, he was partial to terriers, having owned three Airedales before Brandy, and a Fox Terrier prior to that. As a boy he had owned a glorious German Shepherd, who still clearly gripped his emotions. A distant look came over his face whenever he spoke of him, his eyes gazing into the past. This dog (according to Mr. Moore) had been human-like in intelligence, and represented what the German Shepherd used to be, prior to the mess modern breeders had created. The faddish preference for an exaggerated, sloping backline made the dogs prone to hip problems, and over-breeding had diminished their other fine qualities. Mr. Moore felt the only German Shepherds worth owning anymore were bred from strictly German lines.

Through Mr. Moore I began to learn about the world of dog shows. During vacations, the Moores traveled around the western U.S. in their motor home, exhibiting Brandy in the show ring. Brandy was of champion parentage, and a truly impressive specimen. At one large dog show in the previous year Brandy had not only won the Best of Breed, but a fourth-place ribbon in the Terrier Group—quite an achievement. He had the fifteen points needed for a championship, but still needed a "major" win to put him over the top for the AKC requirements. Mr. Moore loved dog showing and clearly enjoyed grooming and preparing Brandy for the competitions, but he was also cynical about the politics involved and the way professional handlers had come to unfairly dominate the sport.

He was an expert dog trainer as well, having been tutored in California under the watchful eye of a disciple of William Koehler, the famous California trainer of dogs for Walt Disney studios. Though Mac was not from show quality bloodlines, I could enter him in AKC obedience competition, and as soon as Mac was six months old, we began working with Mr. Moore to that end. I would walk Mac over to his house in the early evenings after supper, and together we would walk around the neighborhood, me and Mac, Mr. Moore and Brandy. We had several spots with open space where we would stop and train our dogs. He and Brandy were also working on a Companion Dog title (C.D.), having already earned a Tracking Dog title. We practiced walking at heel, on and off leash, sitting, standing still, laying down, staying and coming on command.

Under his tutelage, Mac and I developed into quite a team. Later that year, we enrolled in training classes at the Upper Snake River Valley Dog Training Club, so that Mac could get used to being around other dogs. I was mesmerized at those classes, as I saw gathered there so many of the dog breeds I had only seen in books. I would walk up to owners and breathlessly ask questions I already knew the answer to, such as, "Is that a Borzoi? Is that a Soft-Coated Wheaten Terrier? Is that a Belgian Tervuren?" People seemed impressed that a boy of my age was able to name so many breeds.

Entering the noisy gymnasium where the classes took place was a mystical experience. I left the dull outside world behind, and stepped into the holy sanctuary of dog fanciers. I can still hear the sound of sneakers squeaking across the floor, and dogs barking with excitement as owners strain on the other end of the leash. The metallic choke chain used for obedience training makes a distinct noise when tugged on, and that sound still resonates deeply within my psyche. I was overwhelmed, practically trembling with energy, joy and pleasure, every time I crossed the threshold into that building. It was like I had entered a fantasy world that had scarcely seemed real to me in the pages of my books at home.

At the end of the class, after some weeks had passed, Mac and I won a first place trophy at graduation, with a nearly perfect score in the Novice competition. I can still remember the glowing look on Mr. Moore's face as I stepped forward to receive my prize, tears in his eyes, full of pride, like a father admiring a son. Mac had performed for me with poise, his face full of love and excitement as he looked up at me, awaiting my commands. And I in turn had performed for Mr. Moore, my face full of hope as I glanced in his direction. I felt like I was picking up a mantle that had been passed down the line from the famous William Koehler himself. Clearly I was destined for greatness in the dog ring. Over the course of the following year we picked up the three scores necessary to earn the C.D. title at local obedience trials sponsored by the AKC.

Our success attracted some notice from local dog fanciers, and one day I was contacted by a local breeder of Basenjis. She wanted to give me a show quality Basenji puppy that I could train and show in addition to Mac. Apparently she was convinced that I had tremendous potential and a promising future in the world of dogs. She even brought the puppy over to the house for me to see and I desperately wanted to accept her offer, but my mother insisted that we could not afford to take care of more than one dog. At the end of the day I had to thank the kind lady for her offer, but decline. I was sullen and heart-broken at the time, but looking back on it, given the course my life would take, it was the right decision.

Another person who came into my life at this time was Jean Pugh. Whereas Richard Moore first introduced me to the world of dog training and obedience trials, Jean Pugh's interest lay mostly in the conformation ring, where dogs are judged according to their conformity with AKC breed standards. She raised and showed Doberman Pinschers. Years earlier she had owned a large breeding operation (a puppy mill essentially) named Tradewind Kennels, and now the brand name of Tradewind was attached to the Dobermans she bred.

Jean was a short, plump woman in her sixties, with a bumpy nose, who would have made a good witch had a pointy black hat been placed on her head. Her husband had died a decade or so earlier, and I think she was quite lonely, and a little bitter at the end of the day.

I came into contact with Jean through Ruth Hudson, who, for some reason, had known her for years. Ruth seemed to have contacts with every important person in the Idaho Falls area. Jean operated a small grooming business out in Ammon, and one day she called to invite me to come over and spend some time at her small house on a Saturday afternoon, and watch her groom the dogs. I listened to her on the phone, describing the many breeds she had owned over the years, and eagerly accepted her offer. When I eventually mentioned to Richard Moore that I had met Jean Pugh, he seemed well acquainted with her, but was less than flattering in expressing his opinion of her.

"Yeah, I know that bitch," he said, as I looked at the ground, biting my lower lip.

Nonetheless, she seemed to be treating me kindly for the time being at least, and I soon became fond of my visits to her home on Saturdays, especially as her shelves were stocked with fascinating books about purebred dogs, the history of various breeds, and the ins and outs of dog breeding, dog training and dog showing. Plus she had six or seven Doberman Pinschers running around the place.

Between Jean and Mr. Moore, I was getting a lot of exposure to the world of purebred dogs during my sixth and seventh grade years. For the first time in my life I began to get a sense of purpose, identity and possible vocation. For awhile I was convinced I wanted to be a veterinarian, but as the months went by my focus shifted. Almost from the time I attended my first dog show, I knew I wanted to divide my life between dog training for obedience competition, and professional handling in the conformation ring. Though Mac (the produce of a backyard breeder) was not a "show quality" specimen of his breed, I attended the dog handling classes sponsored by the Eagle Rock Kennel Club anyway, just to learn the techniques of exhibiting a dog in the show ring.

The classes were taught by a man who exhibited Shih Tzus and was well known nationally on the show circuit. He had a flamboyant way about him, and Jean informed me that he was gay. He is the first gay person that I can ever recall having a conversation with. He was very kind and helpful, and encouraged me about Mac's conformity to the breed standard. Though apparently his coat texture, gait and size were all insurmountable problems for the show ring, as was the fact that his ears were not cropped, he told me that Mac's head was a nearly perfect example of what a Miniature Schnauzer head should look like according to the breed standard.

He pointed out to me the shape and slope of Mac's skull and cheek bones, and the way his ears were set proportionally on his head. I was extremely gratified to be told that, and somehow knowing that Mac had a beautiful head made me feel better about the fact that I would not be able to show him in the conformation ring. I was informed though that I could enter him in junior handling competitions, where the issue is the skill of the handler, not the show quality of the dog.

I loved going to the dog shows with Jean and immediately fell in love with every detail of the atmosphere: the food concession stands, the booths where dog products were sold, the show rings themselves and especially the grassy areas where the participants were encamped. The night before the first set of shows I attended, we visited the site. We pulled into the parking lot in Jean's station wagon with about an hour or so of sunlight left in the day. Before my eyes lay a vast sea of motor homes and trailers, sprawled out like a fleet of ships prepared for war.

It was early evening at the tail end of a warm June day, and as we walked among the exhibitors camping there, I saw men and women relaxing outside their vehicles with drinks and cigarettes in their hands. Many were grooming their dogs or sitting in lawn chairs chatting and laughing with friends and fellow dog fanciers. The people there seemed so happy, and the atmosphere was focused and intense in a way I liked. I could think of no other place I would rather be.

Breeds of every imaginable variety were resting in kennels and cages as far as the eye could see. There was an excitement and anticipation in the air, a buildup of drama in view of the ring battles that would take place the following day between old foes and friendly competitors. As I surveyed my surroundings I just knew that one day I would be sitting there among them, preparing and strategizing for the next day's competition, while enjoying a relaxing evening with friends as the sun crawled down the horizon.

I began attending the monthly meetings of the Eagle Rock Kennel Club regularly. Sitting there at the local restaurant with Jean and the other members, eating my food and listening to the discussions of club business point by point, made me feel something I had found nowhere else in my twelve years of existence. I felt welcome among these people, like I had been placed in a family, in the midst of a broader set of connections to others with whom I shared a common bond.

I belonged.

I mattered.

I found something among them I did not experience in my loosely linked network of relatives, nor among the Mormons with whom I sojourned on Sundays. I said very little at the meetings, but I basked in the warmth of their fellowship like a tourist reclining on the sand of a Florida beach, feeling glad just to be there. Finally, the world was beginning to make sense.

Dark Clouds Approach (1982-1983)

The summer between my sixth and seventh grade years was a magical time. Terry, my mother, Mac and I spent a week in a cabin at Mack's Inn, in Island Park, Idaho. Mack's Inn is nestled near the western border of Yellowstone National Park, and it is a wonderful place to be. Terry and my mom divided their time between reclining in chairs outside our cabin and sitting on the spacious front porch of the general store, playing cards and visiting with other guests.

I was in heaven, surrounded by a natural paradise. Songbirds chirped, flitting about in the sunshine and busying themselves with gathering items scattered in the parking area. The pine trees from the surrounding forests filled the air with a wild fragrance. Mac was by my side, panting happily and taking in the scenery, as we sat on the front porch steps of the general store. There was a lovely river nearby, visited by moose in the mornings and evenings, much to the delight of the camera-wielding tourists. Across the road beyond the store were rustic cabins. Vacationers would drive by on the highway, pickups carrying camper shells and pulling boats, headed to Yellowstone and nearby places.

I loved to walk down to the river. The water made a calm swooshing noise as it moved along the rocky shoreline. I can still hear the sound of the water and the happy voices of people in their boats on the river. Standing on the southern shoreline, I could look quite a ways to the east toward Yellowstone and to the west toward the central Idaho wilderness. Despite the people, it still looked pure and calm, like you wouldn't be surprised to see an Indian in buckskin clothing come floating down the river toward you, serenely moving along the shoreline in his canoe.

Mac always came with me on my jaunts, sniffing along the ground at the exciting smells or looking up at me and panting with a contented look in his eyes. Sometimes we would walk together along the forest trails on either side of the highway, always alert for signs of moose and grizzly bears, both of which inhabited the area. It was not yet heaven, but it was not earth, either; Mack's Inn was caught in mid-air somewhere between this world and the world to come.

When that summer ended, I had to face the seventh grade and the terrors of junior high school. Just shy of twelve, I entered a world of class schedules, popularity contests, bullying, gym class and other adolescent challenges. I was small, easily intimidated at school, and played no sports to make me popular. The friends I had made in the sixth grade scattered to the winds and struggled for their own survival. I pretty much spent my days trying to avoid harassment and the unwanted attentions of those who might find pleasure in my suffering. The first part of the year was very difficult, but my trials were eventually eased by two strokes of fortune.

The first was that a very large ninth grader who played on the basketball team took a liking to me, which kept me safe whenever I was in his presence. He was well acquainted with Richard Moore through his dad, and he put out signals in my gym class (he was a teacher's assistant) for kids to leave me alone. During class I would often practice my footwork in the gymnasium for moving around the dog obedience ring in the heeling exercises, carefully pivoting my feet in certain ways on the corners. My tall advocate asked what I was doing one day, and upon hearing my explanation, he passed it on to the other students, who all nodded their heads in appreciation, and seemed to find it a most worthy pursuit.

The other thing that happened was that I finally stood up to a bully. After tolerating months of harassment, I lost the ability to remain passive one day during social studies class. In the middle of class he had walked over to my side of the room to sharpen his pencil. He then turned to me and, with a flick of his hand, tossed some pencil shavings in my face, and then smugly walked back to his desk. Some of the shavings got in my eyes, which pushed me over the edge I guess.

The scene that followed seemed to take place in slow motion. After wiping the shavings out of my eyes, I got up and walked past the teacher's desk in the front of the class. She studied me with an alert gaze as I traveled over to his desk on the far side of the room. Then, without a word, I proceeded to punch him in the side of the head with great sincerity. He jumped up from his chair, like a startled cat in the middle of a nap, and then in front of the class we put on something of a boxing exhibition.

This was the 1980's, and there were still some teachers left in those days who took a "boys will be boys" attitude toward such things. I distinctly remember our mutual surprise as the teacher actually kept the other students from breaking the two of us up, and said that we needed to "work this out of our system." She let us continue to fight! So we swung wildly at each other, for what seemed like forever, until she finally signaled that we should be broken apart. After that, the rest of my seventh grade at least, passed mostly without incident, and even boys who formerly had taken great delight in tormenting me, now patted me on the back and congratulated me for what I had done.

Then, subtly as the year progressed, things started to change at home in various ways. I noticed that Terry and my mother weren't getting along as well as they used to. The details were never made clear to me, but it would seem my mother had gotten the impression that Terry was trying to somehow "steal me" from her. Whether my mom arrived at that impression herself, or others planted the idea in her head, I am not sure to this day, but, nonetheless, they began to argue a lot, and our duplex was gradually overtaken with a very tense atmosphere. Terry soon moved into an apartment downtown, near the Snake River and the LDS Temple, and I saw very little of her from that point on. After all the memories she shared with me and my mother, I find it sad that she walked out of our life so suddenly, so inexplicably.

The other thing that happened is that, my mother's health began to slowly deteriorate. As the months rolled by, she looked increasingly weary and haggard, as though the aging process in her body was suddenly kicked into high gear by some invisible, passionless hand. She became short-tempered and impatient at home, something that was entirely out of character. And she began to complain about a mysterious ache in her side. I became increasingly alarmed at her deteriorating health.

Then something bizarre and tragic took place within our family, which to this day I am at a loss to explain. After a doctor's visit one afternoon, Ruth Hudson and my aunt Bonnie took me aside and explained to me that my mother's symptoms were all in her head, and that her complaints were only an attempt to get our sympathy and attention. The best thing I could do for her, they said, would be to ignore her when she spoke about these pains and aches in her body. Outwardly I went along with it, but inwardly I was skeptical. They didn't live with my mother. There was something about the earnestness in her moaning and tears that told me this was far more than her imagination.

Time passed, and passed, and her health continued to worsen week by week. Then one evening I was sitting in the living room watching television with Mac when suddenly I heard an awful crash and a scream in the hallway. I ran to the scene and saw her there on the floor, her voice full of tears and agony. I knelt down beside her and asked what had happened, and between her sobs and gasps she told me that something had broken. Medical tests would show that her hipbone had fractured under the weight of her step, as she was gingerly making her way down the hall. I called Ruth on the phone in a panic and explained to her what had just happened. Ruth rushed over to the house, an ambulance was called, and my mom was whisked away to the hospital.

And so, just like that, my serene little world came to a crashing end. Tests proved that she had been suffering with cancer for some time, and it had spread throughout her stomach and hip. I can remember sitting in the hospital room as the doctor announced his diagnosis.

"She has a tumor in her stomach," he said with a serious expression.

The word "tumor" was slightly unfamiliar to me, but it gave me a shiver, and I had a sense of what the word conveyed. Tears began to well up in my eyes as I sought clarification of what I already knew in my heart.

"You mean she has cancer?"

The doctor nodded sadly, and I immediately burst into tears as the dam to my emotions was breached. I also learned that her normal bowel functions were affected, and so now they had to take the measure of attaching a colostomy bag to her side.

After a couple of weeks, she was allowed to return home, and I was charged with tending to her needs and helping her change her colostomy bag. At twelve years of age, I simply wasn't prepared emotionally to deal with the reality of the sights and smells involved, though I did what I could. Ruth and Bonnie came to the house to offer assistance. I can remember very little from those final months at the duplex. It only lasted until the end of the summer.

One other experience from this same time period does stand out, though I can't recall if it was just before, or sometime after, my mother's diagnosis with cancer. But suddenly she announced her desire to "go to church." She had not darkened the halls of a church building for years so far as I was aware, though the Mormons continued to send well-meaning women from the "Relief Society" to visit her at home on a regular basis. When she announced this wish, by her choice of wording I knew it was not the Mormon Church that she had in mind; she wanted to attend a *Protestant* service. Somehow, she located the worship schedule of a local Lutheran congregation, and one hot Sunday morning we made our way across town to attend. Though it would have been a short drive in a car, on foot it was still quite a distance for us. We didn't have a car, and my mother couldn't drive anyway.

We arrived eventually, tired and sweaty, the difficulty of my mother's journey no doubt increased both by her natural handicap, and the toll her struggle with cancer was already taking on her body. We had underestimated the amount of time it would take us to get there, and by the time we arrived the service had already started. We were both lost within the structure of their liturgy, never experiencing anything like it in the Mormon Church. But at least we stayed until the service was over. Nobody said a word to us, or even seemed to notice our presence. I can only imagine what the two of us must have looked like in that setting.

My mother was very quiet, bearing a defeated demeanor as we wearily made our way home under the glare of the merciless summer sun. As we trudged along, I made it clear I had no intention of returning to that place.

"What a stupid church," I muttered with a scowl. "Why did you make us go there?" She said nothing, and never brought up the subject again.

Years later, I would discover a letter written to my mother from my father at the VA hospital in his last days, in which he told her of his conversion to a Protestant faith at the end of his life.

By the time my eighth grade year rolled around, my mom had been moved to the Good Samaritan nursing home. Her condition was worsening and she was no longer able to receive sufficient care at home. Mac and I moved in with my aunt and uncle, Bonnie and Norman Hunting. They lived in a singlewide trailer in Ammon, out on the eastern outskirts of Idaho Falls. The setting was rural, consisting mostly of farmer's fields, trailer courts and country homes.

My favorite haunt was the field which lay along the northern edge of the trailer park. I walked there often with Mac, especially in the winter, always alert for the tracks of rabbits, field mice, and the occasional fox. Knowing that some elusive creature had stood in that very spot ignited my imagination. *Where was it now? Was it aware of me?* Watching me perhaps, from some quiet place, as I studied the trivia of its journey with wonder?

The Huntings were a very quiet couple in their forties, beaten down by the challenges of living just north of the poverty line all their lives. Bonnie worked as a nurse's assistant at the nursing home where my mother was staying. Uncle Norman was a mechanic at a potato-processing factory just north of town. Bonnie was short and stocky, with reddish blond hair, and tended to look down at the floor most of the time with a glazed expression, or distantly to the side and slightly down when being spoken to. Norman was even shorter than Bonnie, built like a horse jockey, and was actually the quieter of the two. He generally expressed himself with observations; rarely did he ask questions or engage in humor. His tersely worded statements usually began with a drawn out "Yep," when he chose to speak.

"Yep, cain't remember the last time we got this much rain in July." Or, "Yep, ya can only drive that aways for so long."

Mac and I settled into their small trailer with little fanfare. I knew

Bonnie and Norman fairly well from family reunions and other visits, so I was comfortable with them. They had some curious rules though.

Bathing was only allowed once a week; more than that was simply a waste of water. This was not helpful to an adolescent boy with a greasy hair. Purchasing shirts and pants from a store, was likewise seen as a waste of money. Bonnie insisted on sewing together such items from cheap materials she could buy for herself. Furthermore, water was not to be wasted by washing clothes too frequently. So Bonnie sewed together *two sets* of clothing. Upon returning home from school, I was immediately to change into my "home" shirt and pants. That way I could wear the same clothes all week at school without them getting too soiled, since after all, I only had them on half the day. The fact that I consequently wore the same clothing nearly every day at school, throughout the year, certainly did not go unnoticed by my classmates.

My contacts with Richard Moore naturally became infrequent once I moved to Ammon. Back when my mother had first been diagnosed, I had spoken with my school counselor (a heavy-set, bearded man with soft, kind eyes) about my affection for Mr. Moore, and expressed the wish that perhaps, I could go and live with the Moores rather than my aunt and uncle if my mother were to pass away. The counselor set up an appointment, bringing Mr. Moore into the school to speak with me. Obviously he felt this was an important desire that I needed to give expression to, and bring out into the open to deal with.

So one day Mr. Moore came in and sat down in our meeting room. By the sad expression on his face I knew that he was already aware of what I was going to ask him, and I already knew by that same expression what his answer was going to be. But I asked anyway.

I pointed out what a good friend and father figure he had become for me, how well we got along, and how attached I had become to him and his wife Betty. I added into the equation the affection that our dogs Brandy and Mac clearly had for each other, and how Mac had almost become like a little brother for Brandy. Given all these things, and my mother's deteriorating health, I wondered, if there would be any possibility of me coming to live with them when my mom died.

Mr. Moore's eyes welled up with tears as he listened to my pleas without interruption. And then he began to speak. He explained to me that I had become like a son to him, and that I meant a great deal to him and his wife. And they adored Mac dearly, and knew that Brandy would love for Mac to come and stay with them. But, he and Betty were well into their sixties, and at this stage in their lives, they simply could not take on the responsibility of raising me, however much they might wish they could. They were just too old, he said, to adjust to the sorts of challenges raising a teenager would pose. At the end of the day, it would be best for me to go and live with my aunt and uncle.

We all cried, and blew our noses with napkins, but there it was. The Moores would not be offering Mac and me a safe haven. My fairy tale ending to the story, like most of our fantasies in this life, would forever remain just that.

My contacts with Jean Pugh continued though, both before and after my mother's death. If anything, they became even more frequent as time marched on. I still went to her house for visits, only now the relationship gradually changed. Rather than just stand there and watch her groom the dogs, or quietly spending the time sitting with a dog magazine, I was now asked to perform various tasks for her. In gratitude for all she had done, and continued to do for me, surely I wouldn't mind stacking her firewood, mowing her grass, cleaning the infinite piles of dog poop from her large back yard, where her Dobermans were kept, or performing whatever job was suited to the season and needs of the moment. And, as it turns out, a darker side of Jean's personality began to reveal itself.

One time I was helping her brush out the mats in the hair of a dog she was grooming, when suddenly she snatched the wire brush out of my hand and brought it down across my scalp in a vicious, scraping motion. I stood there, wide-eyed and astonished, rubbing the bloody spot on the top of my head.

"Doesn't feel very good, does it?" she asked. Apparently this was her way of indicating I needed to be gentler in working the mats out with the brush.

On another occasion, we were driving to one of the local hospitals to visit with my mother, in the weeks before she was put into the nursing home. At one point in the journey she turned to me in the car and said, "You know, I hate to say this Paul, but you deserve to watch your mother die. You've been a terrible son."

Still struck and stunned by the hurt of those words, I had little appetite for conversation during the hospital visit, and Jean made sure to point out to me what a *rude* young man I was, as we made our way back to the car afterwards. I was deeply depressed and sullen by this point, responding only with shrugs, yet she engaged me in small talk during the drive home, as though nothing had happened.

We drove past a field where some horses were grazing, and she commented on them. When I said nothing in return, she furiously hit the breaks, turned and slapped me hard across the side of the face. "You ungrateful little brat," she spat, her eyes blazing with anger. I said nothing as I wiped tears away and stared out the passenger-side window for the rest of the ride home. I remember fences, fields, hopeless, helpless.

A Cold Night in November (1983)

===

I can still recall the day of my mother's passing.

It's the first week of November, and in Idaho, that usually means cold weather. The landscape is tense, bracing itself for nature's fury, which will be meted out over the coming winter months. In Idaho Falls, people are busying themselves with activity. They walk briskly from their cars into stores and shopping centers, buying early Christmas gifts and other necessities of life. As night falls, the city is lit up beautifully, in anticipation of the coming holiday season. People sit in traffic with their families and discuss important matters, like elk hunting, shopping, sports, snowmobiling and homework. Teenagers are preoccupied with the important power struggles of the wrestling and basketball seasons in the local high schools.

In the very center of the city, along the northern edge, lies the Good Samaritan nursing home. There, inside one of the rooms, my mother is lying very still on her bed, dying. No longer does she cling to her life like a treasure; she is eager to let it go. Like a defeated boxer inside the ring, wearied by the opponent's punches, she leans against the ropes, ready to fall to the canvas at any moment. The cosmic referee has seen enough, and tonight, he will jump in and wave the contest off.

Inside her room, a small group has gathered to see her one last time, before her 49-year-old journey is brought to its end. Ruth Hudson is there, as are two of her sisters, Bonnie Hunting and Marie Tolley. Nurses quietly come in and out. My mother is very quiet tonight, and can no longer speak, but she is conscious and faintly aware of her surroundings.

What exactly is going on in the drug induced state of mind under which she hovers in those final hours? Nobody will ever know for sure. If she is at all distressed by this crisis, this facing-down of the inevitable, she is unable to show it.

I can surmise with some likelihood that her final thoughts are directed on me.

What will become of Paul?

She knows by now, from hard experience as a single mother, that I can be difficult to manage at times.

Will he adjust well to living with Bonnie and Norman?

Would he have been better off living with Marie and Howard in Blackfoot?

Will he be able to stay out of trouble?

My mother maintained a sincere, though theologically fuzzy belief in God and Jesus Christ to the end. The Mormon Church taught her that much in her childhood, growing up in the pioneer-settled Upper Snake River Valley, though in her adult years she had avoided church attendance. I wonder what it is like for an insecure, physically handicapped, single mother, with tattered clothing, to sit through a typical Mormon service? I think I understand her choice to stay home.

Regardless, she had encouraged me to pray throughout my childhood, especially before going to sleep at night. When I was little, she used to pray with me at my bedside.

"Now I lay me down to sleep. I pray the Lord my soul to keep. If I should die before I wake, I pray the Lord my soul to take."

I can imagine her, in those final hours, praying in her hazy stream of consciousness. Is she praying for me, there on that hospice bed, as she lays helpless and stretched out, like Jesus prayed for wayward sinners on the cross? Does she pray that God would keep me in his care, and help me to enjoy a better life than she was able to secure?

Am I typing these words from a comfortable office in North Carolina, precisely because of the heartfelt prayers of a dying mother?

It's getting late, and someone in the room tells me that my mother is very sick, and that it is important that tonight, I say whatever is in my heart to her while I have a chance.

The time has come to say goodbye.

So, I quietly approach her bedside and lean over her. I put my face very close to hers, and place her small hand in my hand for the last time. Her face is freakishly swollen and disfigured, whether from the medicine or the disease, I do not know. Her eyes are closed, and she breathes with a kind of resolute weariness that signals her imminent departure from the world.

"Mom. It's me, Paul. Can you hear me? If you can hear me, squeeze my hand." (She does.) I take a deep breath and choke back tears. A deep ache is welling up from my stomach and working its way in waves through my adolescent frame.

"Mom, I just want you to know that I love you very much. I'm so sorry for all the mean things I ever said to you. You are the best mom in the world, and I didn't mean to say anything to hurt you. You do know I love you very much don't you?" (Again, she squeezes my hand.) "And I just want you to know that I'm going to be okay. I'm going to be just fine. I don't want you to worry about me, okay?"

With that, I kiss her on the forehead, and pause to stroke her black hair with my fingers. After some tearful embraces with others at the scene, I leave my mother behind in the room.

In the blackness and chill of the winter night my aunt Bonnie drives me back to their trailer home in Ammon. There my uncle Norman and my beloved Mac, who has been eagerly awaiting my return, sympathetically greet me. At some stage, I take Mac into my room and fall asleep. I am awakened a few hours later, probably at 3 or 4 in the morning. My aunt and uncle have opened the door and flicked on the bedroom light.

I look up from the bed, eyes blinking, and know in that instant that my mother is gone. My aunt sits down on the edge of the bed. Unsure what to say in a moment like this, she is only able to utter one word.

"Paul . . ."

I reach out reflexively, and stroke my hand over the back of my dog as everyone in the room bursts into tears.

Life in an Ammon Trailer (1983-1984)

A day or two after my mother died, I was told that we were going to see her body at the funeral home. The suggestion seemed logical enough at the time, but as Bonnie drove me to the location, I began to have second thoughts. A gradual sense of terror started to build up within me, as I thought of the prospect of being confronted with her lifeless corpse. It's not that I didn't really know she was dead without seeing the evidence; it's just that there was a terrible finality about actually coming face to face with her, in that state of death. The thought of being there with her physically, but not being able to interact with her, knowing I could talk but she would not hear my voice, began to turn my world upside down the closer we came to the mortuary. I started to feel overwhelmed with emotion and insecurity.

Ruth Hudson was there to meet us. As we all walked from the parking lot to the entrance, I changed my mind. As we passed through the front door I stopped.

"You go on ahead. I think I'm just going to wait in the car," I said, staring blankly in all directions.

Ruth insisted that this was not an option. She told me I would regret it if I didn't face up to the reality of this death. Ruth had been a military nurse during World War II and was well acquainted with death; apparently she was much more comfortable in its presence than I was at the age of 13. She grabbed my hand as though to reassure me, but her grip was firm and strong. I began to cry and plead with them to let me go back to the car, but Ruth had a firm grasp of my hand and pulled me further into the building, with Bonnie now holding onto my other arm to prevent me from breaking free. I yanked and pulled, until finally I accepted that there was no way for me to escape, and submitted to the inevitable.

I walked up to her open casket. My mother was clothed in a pretty blue dress and shoes that made her look like she was headed to a ballroom dance. Her closed eyes and still features gave something of the appearance of sleep, but not quite. The body of a sleeping person gives off subtle signs of life, even if breathing very lightly, but the skin on my mother's face and hands was eerily held in place. It was almost as if I wasn't looking at my mother at all, but only a still picture of her. She was lifeless and absent in the same way as a person is in a photograph. It was her, but yet it was not her at all; only a glimmer of the person she had been.

I reached out and touched her forehead and cheeks, which were cold and waxy in texture. In those tangible moments I was confronted with the reality of what I already knew, but in a different sort of way; that my mother, the real person I had known from birth, was no longer there for me to reach out to. She could offer me no love or protection, no comfort or advice, no counsel or sympathy, no matter how I might long for it. I looked up at Ruth to indicate that I had seen enough, and after a few brief words with the mortician, we walked back out into the chilly November air.

The next order of business was to find some clothing for me to wear to the funeral. I owned nothing remotely resembling dress clothes. Even at the Mormon Church growing up I had always worn casual clothing. But this was a unique occasion—the funeral of my own flesh and blood mother. This called for special measures.

So, Bonnie took me to a local second-hand store to find something appropriate to wear. She picked out for me some dress pants, a long-sleeved shirt, a dress jacket, clip-on tie and some dress shoes. "My aren't you handsome?" she said, as I came out of the dressing room and stood awkwardly in front of a mirror.

I had a strange mixture of feelings upon putting on these "new" clothes. On the one hand, I almost felt wealthy. I had never owned such articles of clothing before. On the other hand, the jacket and shoes were noticeably a couple of sizes too big. The sleeves hung down to my fingers, and the whole jacket felt large and bulky. My feet slipped loosely in and out of my heavy maroon dress shoes. People would notice.

The day of the funeral was miserable. My newly purchased shoes soon caused blisters. I stood around quietly in the corners and hallways by myself, with nobody to talk to, and nothing in particular to say. I took in the sniffs and whispers of relatives and family friends. People looked at me with sympathy and shook their heads while saying things like, "He's lost both of his parents now, the poor thing."

I felt strangely disconnected from all those people. I knew they cared in varying degrees about my loss and the tragedy of my mother's death. *But would any of them really be there for me? If I picked up the phone and called, would they offer advice, money, or a place to stay?*

And so I was marched wearily into the next phase of my life. I settled into my daily routine with Norman and Bonnie Hunting in their trailer in Ammon. Things began to change almost immediately. After my mother passed away, Norman announced that Mac could not live inside any longer. He built a kennel for Mac to live in outside.

From the time he was a puppy, Mac had always lived indoors and slept with me on my bed, but now that was gone. When the weather was warm enough in the summer months, I slept outside in my tent and sleeping bag so that we could stay together, but a piece of my heart died that first night I had to leave Mac behind. I could feel his curious brown eyes watching me as I walked away. I would get up in the mornings and visit with Mac before school as he bounced up on his hind legs to greet me, assuring him of my love, but unable to care for him properly. The glimmer began to go out of my eyes as I watched everything around me that I cared for suffer.

That winter of 1983-1984 was exceptionally cold, with temperatures reaching 50 degrees below zero. In Iona, not far from where we lived, herds of elk were starving. Haunting images of them, freezing and worn down by malnutrition and the merciless reality of nature, were played regularly on the TV news. The elk found some measure of food and protection from the elements thanks to the cooperation of local farmers and the Idaho Fish & Game department. It was a frequent topic of conversation that year.

I especially remember that winter. The cold temperatures that hung in the air in the mornings, the warmth and smells of the wood-burning stove, the sound and feel of frozen snow crunching underfoot while walking from the bus into school, the scenery to the east that greeted me as I dreamily looked out my classroom window toward the snow-covered hillsides and the Teton mountain range.

When I would get up for school in the mornings, Norman would already be up, sitting at the kitchen table while smoking a cigarette and listening to the country music station, as the engine of his Ford truck warmed up in their makeshift garage. Lyrics such as "Roll on eighteen wheeler, roll on!" and other pleasant tunes with lines such as "She's in love with the boy!" added a regular rhythm to my daily routine. He said little to me in the mornings or otherwise.

Sometimes, even in the winter, he would work on his pickup truck outside, often long after dark, and have me come out there with him to hold a light, or hand him particular tools while he worked. I never got the sense that he had me there for the company. I was there because he felt a man needed to learn these skills, and this was his attempt to pass the knowledge on to me. I rarely felt very inquisitive about what he was doing with the truck though. I had no intentions of engaging in such activities once I got older. And I think that annoyed him.

One interest which Norman had, which did get my attention however, was deer hunting. I was spellbound by his description of his hunting trips over the years, and his experiences with wildlife. It seemed to strike a chord between us.

Almost.

I can vividly remember one evening, when he asked if I had a minute as I was about to retire to my bedroom. He then went to the back of the trailer and emerged with his two deer rifles: a .30/06 and a .30/30. He sat down and explained, to my utter fascination, the physical features and ballistic characteristics of these guns, and what types of game they were suited for.

From that point on I made a habit of checking out books on hunting and wildlife from the library whenever I could, and purchased outdoor magazines whenever I had spare money. I remember the bliss I would derive when a new issue of *Field & Stream* or *Peterson's Hunting* would arrive on the stand at the local convenience store. I would bring my magazines home and lay on the floor, stretched out with the lights low, the heat from the wood-burning stove providing a wonderful warmth. Alone with my thoughts, I would read about tactics for elk hunting, where trophy mule deer were likely to be found in the fall, and what rifle calibers were best suited for each type of game animal. I never thought of hunting in terms of killing wild animals for sport; even as a teen that mentality repulsed me. I saw it as an attempt by man to maintain a connection with nature. When I tried to convey that notion to my uncle, he seemed to affirm in principle that this was important, though he more or less saw it in very practical terms as an opportunity to secure a good supply of meat for the freezer.

My contacts with dog fanciers became less frequent upon moving into the trailer, though I did continue to attend some shows and events with Jean Pugh. Norman and Bonnie were not going to support my interest in the hobby, that much was clear. There were fees involved in registering for dog shows, plus the cost of supplies and other expenses. So, my hopes of being a professional dog handler and trainer soon began to fade away in the light of reality. Whenever I did get the chance to attend a dog show, I volunteered for the kennel club, cleaning up dog poop in the rings or working in the concession stands in exchange for a meal ticket. That at least allowed me the opportunity to be there and soak up the delicious environment.

A curious incident took place around this time though, which could have taken my future in a different direction. The Shih Tzu exhibitor from the local dog club and his partner (also an accomplished exhibitor) took an interest in my plight. At some point I spoke with him about my fading ambitions to be a dog handler, and he made an offer to allow me to travel with them around the show circuit that summer, learning to groom and handle dogs and establishing contacts in the trade.

I brought the proposal to my aunt and uncle, who considered it for a day or so. I think the offer was tempting to them, as it would relieve them of the responsibility of feeding and caring for my needs for a few months. But ultimately, no doubt after weighing the obvious sexual orientation of these men, they told me they didn't feel comfortable letting me travel around the country with people they didn't know.

I was deflated. It was like they were conspiring against me, doing everything possible to crush my ambitions. I went to my room to sulk. From the window I could see Mac sitting out in his dog pen, staring into the emptiness.

Was this all that lay ahead for us?

As the months and years rolled by I often looked back and wondered how different my life might have been, had I been allowed to spend that summer on the show circuit. Maybe that gay dog handler did have mixed motives in inviting an attention-starved teenage boy to travel with them in their motor home around the country. More likely though, it was just a genuine gesture, an attempt to offer hope to a promising young dog lover whose prospects for success in this world were obviously slipping away.

We rarely had visitors at the trailer, though there were a few exceptions. Bonnie's (and my mom's) stepfather, whom we all called Grandpa Frank, dropped by every so often from nearby Blackfoot. Grandpa Frank, who had married my mother's mom after my biological grandfather's death, was an extremely good-natured old man, of Native American descent, who always treated me well. At social gatherings with relatives, when I might be off by myself somewhere, sitting against a fence or tossing rocks into a canal, he would saunter up and talk with me about casual things. I always got the sense he preferred the simple and sincere banter of children to the mundane conversations of adults.

He was fond of singing, *"Que sera, sera, sera, whatever will be, will be,"* as he walked into or out of a room. As a young man he had worked for the railroad, and he could always tell you stories about hobos and the various incidents he had witnessed on the trains during the Great Depression. He was kind to Mac, and animals in general from everything I could gather of him. I remember him telling me how disgusted he was with a train conductor who had intentionally run over a moose on the tracks. This was back in the 40's or 50's, yet the memory lingered with him in his old age, still indignant at the crime.

Sandy Birch was their daughter, and she and Keith were also regular guests at the trailer, with their three quiet kids. For some reason I always got excited when their pickup truck would pull into the driveway, even though I was scared of Keith. I could sometimes get him to engage me in conversations surrounding my newly found interest in deer hunting and rifle calibers. Keith hunted with a .308, though he granted it was not as effective at longer ranges as the .30/06.

Keith's tendency toward physical roughness didn't abate as I grew older, and often I would receive a sharp punch to the arm or shoulder as I approached him with a question, or a slap on the back of the head when I attempted to join in a discussion he would be having with Norman. Sometimes he would keep his hands to himself, and hit me verbally with a comment like, "What the hell are you looking at?" as I walked toward him. Or he might stare at me and say, "Who the hell invited you to sit down?" as I quietly took a place alongside the men at the kitchen table.

Co-existing with Keith inside the trailer resembled the scenes you witness on nature programs, as dominant wolves growl and savage their inferiors around the carcass of a fresh kill. Weaker pack members are allowed to feed only after displaying adequate signs of submission. Keith's hostility contrasted with the behavior of my aunt and uncle. Keith's abuse reminded me that I was there at least, that my presence was noticed by others around me.

Norman and Bonnie Hunting were the first of seven foster families I would live with over the next four years. So it fell upon them to teach me a lesson I would have to learn if I was to adjust to foster care. That lesson is simply this.

A foster home is not a family.

The foster kid is not even a domestic pet, which will be showered with affection and scraps from the kitchen table. He exists like those semi-wild dogs whose presence is tolerated on the outskirts of villages in remote Third World countries.

Apart from occasional conversations about guns and his hunting stories, Norman showed no interest in exploring topics that were important to me. He did not care in the least bit about my dog Mac. He had no curiosity about how my day might have gone, or what I was reading lately, or what girl at school I liked, or what my hopes for the future might be. He displayed no concern over how I was coping with the death of my mother, my progress in my classes or the daily challenges of adolescent life.

Norman Hunting said nothing as Keith made it his regular habit to punch, slap and demean me whenever we were in the same room. I was Leona's son, the nephew who stayed in their trailer. And, as long as they received their monthly check from the state for my foster care, that was fine with them, for the time being.

As for Bonnie, she evidenced little interest in much of anything around her, other than her own daily struggle for sanity. When she was not at work, she spent quiet hours lying around the trailer on her bed, in her bathrobe, with her Harlequin romance novels, which offered an escape from her dull life with the man she had married as a teen. I never found it possible to engage her in meaningful conversations. Like Norman, she showed no interest.

As time went by, I gradually learned to live out my day-to-day existence in relative safety from the sanctuary of my bedroom, where I could hide from the uneasy feeling that I now resided as a refugee in a foreign land. From the seclusion of my room, I could avoid the sense that I was taking up extra space, space so valuable, in their trailer, to which I had no right. If I could just avoid their attention for the bulk of the day, apart from meals and other necessary appearances, I thought, perhaps, they would continue to tolerate my presence in their midst. I was wrong.

Tensions and Conflicts (1984)

And so things went as the months rolled on by. There were some
good times. The Huntings owned three old snowmobiles that they
were fond of taking out for winter adventures, and those weekend trips
were without a doubt the highlight of my stay with them. I especially
loved the drives coming and going from the recreation sites, as I took in
the beautiful snowy scenery of the eastern Idaho landscape. I loved, and
always will love, the sight of sagebrush in the snow. But riding around
on the snowmobiles was also a lot of fun for me. We would often see
wildlife during those trips, ranging from deer and elk to jackrabbits, all
of which excited me immensely.

During the summer we spent most weekends out in the woods,
cutting and collecting firewood to take us through the winter. Though
I didn't enjoy the labor involved in loading and unloading the logs into
Norman's pickup and wood trailer, I always enjoyed the scenic drives
along the way. When we would stop for a break or for lunch, I would
ask Norman or Keith (who was often with us) important questions such

as, "How many grizzly bears do you think can hear the sound of the chainsaw from where we are right now?"

It was at this time in my life that I received my first kiss and my first cast. My first kiss came from a relative of Keith's. Her name was Gayelynn Birch, and she lived about twenty miles away in Rigby. She was about a year younger than me, the same height but with a more solid, athletic build, and had short brown hair. For some reason she used to accompany Keith's family on their trips to our trailer, and after a couple of visits I started to feel more comfortable around her. One time Gayelynn suggested we play "kiss hide and seek." Apparently, the rules were simple. If the person doing the searching found you, a kiss had to be exchanged. It didn't take too long for me to do the searching, and she seemed more than willing to be found and do the kissing. Soon, as the summer wore on, there was much more kissing than searching taking place.

My first cast was secured through the same route. Running around the yard after dark while playing this game, I stepped in a hole in the lawn and broke my foot. I remember hearing a sickening snap and feeling a burning sensation along the outer edge of my left foot. My aunt and uncle gave me the evening to see how I would fare, but I woke up the next morning with my foot swollen to twice its normal size, and they realized a trip to the hospital was unavoidable. My foot was put in a cast for six weeks, taking me into the first month of the school year.

So the fall rolled around, and I entered the ninth grade at Bonneville High School. I had not found it easy to make many friends since moving to Ammon, though one tall, gangly boy who shared my interest in the outdoors befriended me, and I spent a fair amount of time talking with him at school and on the bus. Mostly I just kept to myself, now and then enduring snide remarks from soulless adolescents about my goofy clothing, and the occasional bullying on the school bus that most small, thin boys who lack self-confidence endure from time to time.

Two incidents took place early in my ninth grade year that changed the course of my future though. The first involved my dog Mac. Over the summer, my aunt and uncle had purchased an expensive, new doublewide trailer, and looking back on the circumstances, I'm sure the heavier mortgage payment put them under a financial crunch. In any event, money became very tight in the Hunting household. No longer able to cope with the payments, Norman sold his beautiful red Ford pickup truck and purchased a much older, ugly yellow Chevy. Only a week or so after buying it, one of the tires flew off while they were driving down the highway, coming back from getting a load of firewood in Island Park with their grandkids. I wasn't with them at the time, but luckily nobody was hurt.

At some point around that time we ran out of dog food at home. I pointed this out to Aunt Bonnie, who told me that as soon as she got paid they would buy him some food, and that it wasn't going to kill "that dog" to skip a few meals. After a couple days of watching Mac go hungry, I decided to take matters into my own hands, and fed him some bologna from the refrigerator. It wasn't a complete container, and in my naiveté I didn't suspect the meat would even be missed. But when Bonnie came home and discovered that the bologna was missing she asked me about it, and I admitted I had fed it to Mac. She grew silent, and seemed to be very agitated about what I had done. When Norman got home from work she immediately spoke to him about it. From my bedroom I could hear her hushed tones as she described to him what had happened.

We ate a tense dinner without much being said, and then Bonnie left to go run an errand somewhere. Norman planned to do some work outside before dark, and was putting on his overalls, as he always did when engaged in tasks at home. I had gone into my bedroom after dinner to read, as was my habit, when Norman came to the door in stocking feet and knocked.

"I need to talk with you for a minute," he said ominously. So I followed him through the living room into the kitchen area. I was a little unsure what he wanted, so I just awkwardly stood there.

"Sit down," he said, gesturing toward the kitchen table. He sat down opposite me and began putting on his work boots. "Bonnie tells me you fed our lunch meat to that dog," he began, not yet looking up from his boots. Then he did glance up and continued, "Is that true?"

I nodded yes, adding, "He hasn't eaten in days." My uncle then sat up straight in his chair and stared at me with a blank expression.

"There's something I need to explain to you, man to man" he offered, without raising his voice at all, though I detected a slight shaking, as though he were controlling his anger. He continued. "You're not our son. You're not a member of this family. The only reason you even live here is as a favor to your mom. But now you've got Bonnie so worried, she's getting an ulcer, because you decided to take food that doesn't belong to you, and feed it to that damn dog. Now I'm only going to tell you this once. If you ever, do anything like that again, your butt will be out on the street before you know what's hit you. Do you understand?"

That was the longest stream of words that I ever heard come out of my uncle Norman's mouth. I nodded my head to indicate that yes, I understood what he was saying. And indeed I did. I looked off to the side with blurred vision as he finished lacing up his boots, rose and zipped up his overalls. He then turned without a word and walked out the back door.

Looking back on it, it occurs to me that Bonnie's ulcer just might have had less to do with me, and more to do with their ongoing financial struggles, which were exacerbated by their decision (perhaps prompted by the government checks they were receiving for my care) to purchase a doublewide trailer they simply could not afford. And perhaps, rather than blame himself for not being able to provide for his household, it was easier to blame the actions of an anxious thirteen-year-old who was worried about his dog. Eventually, after I had moved out, they ended up getting rid of their expensive doublewide, and spent many years living in a camper trailer hooked to their pickup truck.

Another incident that took place not long after this probably sealed my fate. One evening at the trailer, Keith and his family were visiting. Somehow, through the course of events we began to play with a balloon, bouncing it in the air back and forth to one another. At some point, the balloon came into my possession and Keith and I began to playfully tussle over it. Laughing with excitement, I made an escape through the kitchen into the laundry area with my prized possession in hand. Keith chased me into the little room in the back of the trailer and caught up with me, still in a humorous mood as he attempted to recover the balloon. He began tickling me as I lay on the floor, and it slipped out of my grasp and floated over towards my feet, with Keith clutching the air trying to get it back. Somehow, in the midst of the struggle the balloon popped, and suddenly everything changed.

Without a word, Keith gripped the side of my neck firmly to hold me down, as he began to rain down blows upon my head with a sort of fisted karate chop motion. This bore no resemblance to the bullying punches to the arms and shoulders I had many times endured; these hits bore rage and bad intentions. His strikes carried such force they bounced my skull off the floor of the trailer. He probably hit me six or seven times before he stopped.

Never in my life had I taken a beating like that. It was completely terrifying. I lay there stunned for a few seconds, and then began to cry with choking sobs. Keith simply stood up and walked back into the living room. Aunt Bonnie came over to where I was laying to check on me. Seeing no blood, she said, "Come on, you're okay," as she helped me to my feet. I walked back through the kitchen and crossed through the living room area where everyone was sitting, on my way to the safety of my bedroom. Sandy had a smirk on her face, as though her brave husband had just whipped a pugnacious drunk at the bar, but everyone else looked stunned. There was an awkward silence in the trailer, but nobody made an effort to check on me or ask if I was okay as I made my retreat from the battlefield. And nobody said a word to Keith, a thirty-something-year-old man, about bludgeoning a 100-pound boy over the loss of a balloon.

About two weeks later, I heard a knock on my bedroom door. Norman opened it and asked if I could come out so he and Bonnie could speak with me. I sat down with them at the kitchen table. I could sense something important was about to happen. Bonnie sat in silence while Norman explained that they could see I wasn't happy living with them, and they were worried because I seemed so depressed all the time. Furthermore, they had been thinking a lot about their age, about how they were getting along in years, approaching fifty. It had been a long time since they had any teenagers living with them and they were coming to the conclusion that maybe, they were not the people best suited to raise me.

I sat quietly and listened. "We've given this some thought," Norman continued. "You remember your sister Janice, from Oregon? We've spoken with her, and she and her husband Lance said they would love for you to come and live with them."

She was actually my *half-sister* from my father's first marriage. I had first met Janice Whitmore a little over a year earlier. She had come to visit while my mother was struggling with cancer, and that was the first time I had ever laid eyes on her. Apparently, she wanted to meet my mother before she died, perhaps because she represented a connection to our father who would not be available much longer. Maybe she wanted to take the opportunity to ask my mother some questions about my father's final years of life. In any event, she had come, stayed with us for a few days, and then returned to Oregon. Shortly thereafter, they had invited me back to spend a week with them in Oregon. I didn't think much of it at the time, but there was some discussion, even back then, of me coming and staying with them after my mother died. Now, chance would have it, this is exactly where I was headed.

Janice was a hard-working woman in her forties, who was married to a gritty logger named Lance. Lance had a prominent beer belly, which was offset by extremely muscular arms and shoulders. He had a tiny but visible piece of metal lodged in his eyeball which he had never bothered to have removed, as he had little time for doctors and hospitals. They had three grown sons, a college-age daughter and an adopted son named Mitch. Mitch was Native American, about two years younger than me. Heavy set, good natured and intelligent. Though shy with strangers, Mitch loved to laugh and joke around once you secured his approval. We got along great during my week of visiting.

As Norman and Bonnie now announced to me the change that was about to take place, the thought of having Mitch around made me feel less anxious. Though when asked if I had any preferences in the matter, I half-heartedly insisted I would prefer to stay with them, I knew at the end of the day the decision was already made for me. The Ammon trailer was now nothing more than a holding cell, as I awaited my transfer to a new facility.

Reflecting back on that time in my life, I can see it was doomed from the beginning. Norman and Bonnie did not really want me there; they were simply fulfilling an obligation to my mother. I came to them with nothing to offer but additional expenses and my fractured psyche. How different it might have been, had they been able to see me as a soul entrusted to their care, full of potential and promise for the future. What if they had been able to find some space for me in their hearts, larger than the space in their trailer? What if they had appreciated my bookish nature, and my love for animals? Maybe they could have allowed me the small comfort of having Mac nearby in the darkness of the late-night hours, the only living connection to my mother I had left.

I was immersed, not of my own choosing, into an atmosphere tense with financial worries, and the dry, soulless outlook on life that experience had drilled into their collective psyche. They seemed to lack all capacity for hope, imagination and optimism. For people like my aunt and uncle, life was and is little more than subsistence management, in which one learns to keep expectations low and accept the dreary limitations of the real world.

Later that month, Norman and Bonnie Hunting silently loaded me and Mac into their tired old Chevy pickup. In the pre-dawn darkness we began our journey to Boise on the other side of the state, where the Whitmores were to meet us in a restaurant parking lot. Very little was spoken between us as we made our way along the highway. It was as though with every passing mile the emotional distance between us grew wider. From that day forward they would play no significant part in my life. I greeted the sun crawling over the horizon with a mixture of fear and excitement as sagebrush plains gradually gave way to green valleys and productive fields. And so we made our way westward, and into an uncertain future.

Living in La Grande, Oregon (1984-1985)

T he Whitmores were waiting for us in the parking lot outside a
McDonald's restaurant in Boise. As we all climbed out of our
vehicles, I was immediately struck by their large pickup which Lance
used for his logging job. It looked brand new and shiny, and upon
learning that it was a "diesel" it immediately struck me as a privileged
vehicle of some sort. Nobody I had known to that point owned such a
"diesel" truck. It was red and white, with an impressive back seat space
between the cab and the pickup bed. Janice and Lance were there, as
was Mitch, and their daughter Mona. Mona had just recently graduated
from hair-dressing school, and hoped to make a living as a beautician.
She was about eight years older than me, and I quickly developed
something of a crush.

Uncle Norman and Lance seemed to hit it off pretty well, basking
in the sort of quiet kinship which exists between men who have always
worked hard and understand trades like logging, mechanics and so
forth. As they nodded and chatted, I loaded my bags out of the back

of their camper atop the pickup bed and into the truck of my new family.

Soon the time arrived for us to go our separate ways. I was standing there with Mac, holding his leather leash which I had purchased for his obedience training in my hand. Aunt Bonnie gave me a hug, then held my shoulders at arms length and said, "You behave yourself, okay?" as she wiped a tear from her eye. I nodded that I would do so, then without exchanging words gave Norman a stiff hug, scooped Mac up into my arms, and climbed into Lance's shiny, red and white, diesel pickup. During the ride from Boise to La Grande, I feigned sleep as I rested my head heavily into Mona's shoulder. She had a feminine smell that soothed my anxious spirit, and the softness of her frame served as a shelter from the harshness of the recent months. She smelled, and felt, like a better future.

At first, things seemed to go smoothly enough at the Whitmore's. With two years between us, Mitch and I got along well, and shared a room together. That first night we stayed up late into the night hours, lying on our beds and talking about what life was going to be like now that I had joined their family. He told me all manner of gossip about his three older brothers, Lance, Jr. ("Little Lance" as they called him), Jesse, and Tony.

Tony was in his early twenties, and had been discharged from the army for some reason. He had recently had an operation on his knee, and was going to be staying in the bedroom next to us for awhile, until he got back on his feet. Tony was probably the most intelligent of the three older brothers, but he had an affinity for marijuana. He moved in shortly after I arrived, and we got along pretty well.

Tony was something of a gun nut, always reading *Guns & Ammo* magazine, and I enjoyed exchanging trivia about rifle calibers with him. He was a budding artist, bearing a talent which his mother Janice desperately wished he would cultivate rather than his drug habit. He proudly displayed on the wall of his bedroom, a letter from an art school that announced that he had promising art skills. This school was one of those that advertised in magazines, inviting people to send in their sketches of a printed image, to test their drawing ability. Tony showed me the letter and watched to judge my reaction. I nodded with raised eyebrows and an impressed look on my face. Tony of course, would never become an artist, no matter how many flattering form letters he received.

Jesse was a couple of years older than Tony. He was skinny like a skeleton, with thinning, greasy blond hair, beady eyes and buckteeth that gave him something of the appearance of a snake. As I soon learned, he was bitter, mean and sarcastic. His outlook on the world was shaped by all the bullying he endured growing up. Having been mistreated his whole life, he took out his frustrations on others weaker than himself.

On one occasion, Mitch and I had wandered over to his trailer for some reason, when we heard a commotion coming from inside. We snuck over to the window and peaked in on the nightmare. Jesse was yelling at his wife, who was cowering on the floor before him, pleading for mercy. He pulled her to her feet, only to punch her in the stomach as she rose. She buckled over in pain, while muttering something back at him through choking sobs. Unsure what to do, we silently retreated from the ghastly scene.

Lance, Jr. was the most successful and responsible of the sons. He was married, with two daughters and a son of his own. He had followed in his father's footsteps to become a logger. Lance lacked Jesse's mean spirit, and Tony's shiftlessness, yet he did not seem any happier than anyone else in that household. He often seemed distracted, as though something was wearing on his mind. He typically avoided lengthy conversations with anyone. It seemed almost like conversation would interfere with whatever mysteries he was brooding upon within the dark halls of his mind.

Lance, Sr., the scowling patriarch of the clan, was a foreboding figure. He was built like a Neanderthal, with muscular, hairy arms. Earlier in life he had spent some time in jail, after breaking into a shop and stealing some tires he needed for his vehicle. Lacking a car, he had walked to and from the crime scene and then made his getaway . . . in the snow. The police simply followed the tracks from the broken window to his house. Lance cursed a lot, and frequently used violent metaphors when discussing various matters. It would seem that all manner of problems, ranging from politics to child-rearing to family disputes, to the latest item in the news, could be resolved easily if somebody would just "beat the shit" out of somebody. Employing this simple strategy, the world could quickly become a better place. Lance's logging job required him to be up at 3 a.m., and he would return home at 2 in the afternoon. He went to bed at 8, and was not to be disturbed.

I arrived in La Grande late in September, and registered at the local high school. Of all the high schools I ever attended, La Grande High was certainly the toughest. Populated by the children of loggers and other gritty working-class families, it was not a friendly environment. All the boys chewed Copenhagen tobacco, and smoking was so frequent that there was a special area set aside for student use. Every year they held a grudge-match fighting event at the school, in an attempt to curb teenage brawling, under the logic that students would hold their grievances if they had the opportunity to vent them once a year. Instead, everyone fought during lunch and after school, and then fought again at the scheduled event. I decided early on to pick up the tobacco chewing habit, and fight whoever tried to test my boundaries. This latter strategy nearly landed me in several lunchtime brawls, which I somehow managed to avoid through a lot of scowling and bluffing, always refraining from throwing the first punch because my heart was not really in it. Mostly I just wanted to be left alone.

Suddenly I found myself among strangers, hostile strangers many of them. There was nobody in my new environment whose connections reached into my fading past and my previous life with my mother. I had suddenly lost my already tenuous identity and sense of "place" within the broader network of my surroundings.

So, I started chewing Copenhagen, which never failed to make me sick, though I stubbornly persisted in the practice out of peer pressure. Not only the boys at school, but nearly all the men in the Whitmore family chewed constantly. One day I was standing out with Lance, Sr. in the garage, watching him sharpen his chainsaw blade, when I decided to tell him I had started "chewing." He approved of my decision, nodding with a slightly impressed look, as though it went some way toward proving that I was not a latent homosexual after all. I was impressed beyond words as he explained to me that only sissies spit out the tobacco juice; real men swallow the juice and gradually eat the lipful of tobacco as well.

My social studies teacher took an interest in me at school, as he observed my sulking behavior during class, but he didn't get very far with me. He was an interesting character, a man who used to do social work with gangs in California, before moving to Oregon. He would speak to me in fatherly tones, kneeling at my desk, asking me questions about Idaho, while I replied with apathetic shrugs, and tense, gloomy answers, designed to protect my isolation. With every exchange I would retreat further into myself.

The one person who did manage to break down my defenses a bit was an older, red-haired English teacher. One day not long after I arrived I saw a picture of her dog on her desk and blurted out without thinking, "Oh, that's a Belgian Tervuren, isn't it?" Suddenly, a glimpse of my former life flashed before me. My eyes momentarily brightened.

"Why yes," she said, surprised that I recognized the breed. It was rare for me to talk in school, and from then on she used my love of dogs to open up doors of conversation with me. She was especially fond of the author Jim Kjelgaard, who was also a favorite of mine. She encouraged me to cultivate my love for literature, and never failed to say encouraging things in class about my writing and my academic potential. "Excellence," she would say when commenting on my work. "Settle for nothing less."

Life in the Whitmore household was not easy. They seemed to be just as poor as Aunt Bonnie and Uncle Norman. Maybe even poorer. I was rarely bought clothes for school while I was there (if we ever went school shopping I have forgotten the event), and food rations at home were thin. To avoid the cost of milk, we drank powdered milk, and it was disgusting. It tasted like dirty water mixed with glue. I hated pouring it on my cereal in the mornings.

"Bullshit," Lance exclaimed, noticing my displeasure. "If you weren't told that was powdered milk you wouldn't even be able to taste the difference." How wrong he was. There was a huge difference, an infinite gap, between a cold glass of real milk and that gritty water-substance.

There wasn't much to do for amusement around their house, and there was no money to spend. As a result, Mitch and I were left to ourselves to find ways of staying occupied. Unfortunately for his sister Mona, she ended up being one of our primary sources of entertainment.

Shortly after I moved in, she married a somewhat shiftless young man named Joe, who could never seem to hold down a job. But love is blind, and Mona adored him. He was certainly a handsome fellow, thin and muscular, with a Clark Gable mustache and a gentle charm. Having no stable income, the two of them moved into the house and slept in a bedroom toward the back where they could expect to enjoy the sort of privacy newlyweds need. Were it not for me and Mitch, that is. Somehow the romantic affection of this poor young couple brought out in us the basest expressions of voyeurism.

One evening Joe and Mona were sitting out with the family in the living room, watching television. It was about 9 o'clock when the two lovebirds began to exchange knowing glances, and shortly thereafter Joe stood up with a yawn and nonchalantly announced: "Well I'm really beat. I think we're going to hit the sack." At that point, Mitch and I exchanged our own knowing glance. We gave them about 10 minutes, and then acted as though we were going to rummage for some food. Silently we crept from the back entrance of the kitchen to their bedroom door. It was only about 10 feet, but it took us an inordinate amount of time to travel the distance, for we had to stop every foot or so and struggle to hold in our laughter, grabbing one another's arms, biting our bottom lips and wiping the tears from our eyes.

When we got to the door we were not disappointed, for they had already begun their love-making. We stood with our ears pressed against the cheap wooden paneling and took in the sounds, until the melodrama became too much for either of us to bear. We both began to burst into a fit of laughter as we stood there holding our sides. The sounds from the bed switched from moans to curses, and as we turned to run, Joe threw open the door in a fit of rage. Still laughing, we ran back through the kitchen, skirted the living room and rushed into our bedroom, closing the door behind us with Joe still on our heels in his boxer shorts. Unfortunately for the young couple, the other members of the family seemed to find this all rather amusing, and Mitch and I turned it into a regular habit while I was there.

Not too long after I started school in La Grande, I began to experience some bullying in the hallways from some of the older students. They were far too large and intimidating to even consider offering resistance. One afternoon I was making my way down the hall as the group approached me. I tried to avoid them by sticking close to the wall on the opposite side of the corridor, but it did no good.

As they walked by, a large boy, who looked to be a senior, grabbed me by the shirt and pushed me hard against the wall. He had something he needed to say to me. "You're a faggot, you know that? Say it. Say,

I'm a faggot." I stood there stiffly, looking to the side, saying nothing. Then with a few snide remarks about me being a "pussy," and noting with amusement that I was "going to cry," they continued on their way, apparently pleased with themselves.

I silently stood there in the hallway and wondered inwardly what I was going to do. This particular group had singled me out like a pride of lions hunting gazelles, and there was no escaping them. Their predatory instincts were heightened by my vulnerability.

Directly across the hall from where I was standing was a glass trophy-case. For some reason it caught my attention and I walked over to it. Displayed there, were all the trophies the La Grande wrestling team had secured from various tournaments. Awards of various shapes and sizes decorated the display. I scanned up and down the shelves at the gold and silver colors, the engravings, the wrestling figurines atop the trophies. Suddenly it occurred to me that one reason why I was getting bullied was because I was always alone. I had no crowd to mingle with, no herd of students to protect me from wandering predators. I decided then and there I would try out for the wrestling team.

After making some inquiries, I found out when and where wrestling practice was being held. The next day, I showed up in the locker room after school, unsure what lay ahead of me. I had never played sports growing up, apart from dreaded gym class, and the atmosphere was new to me. I timidly walked over to a locker and began to change from my school clothes into a pair of shorts and a t-shirt. I was surrounded by a mix of sights, smells and sounds. Boys cast me sideward glances, as they had never seen me show up at practice before. My ears took in the sound of locker doors opening and closing; the smell of testosterone and teenage angst and sweaty clothing was all around. Everyone was talking in excited tones, jostling each other about and clowning around. Still having no friends at the school, I said nothing, and simply tried to avoid attracting attention.

Wrestling was a big deal at La Grande High School, and most weight classes filled three contested spots: Varsity, Junior Varsity and a third string team consisting mostly of freshmen. I found from the beginning that I really enjoyed the wrestling practices. At least they got me out of the house. I would sit with fascination, sweat dripping off my nose from the exercises, as I watched the coaches and senior wrestlers give demos on the various techniques and skills involved in perfecting moves. We did push-ups and sit-ups and sprints and pull-ups and all manner of tests of will and endurance. I drew encouragement from the fact that I could do all these things. Many of the kids around me had been wrestling since the age of five or six. I now wished my mother had let me have such experiences growing up.

I liked the practice matches we engaged in, as we were lined up along the wall and paired off with boys our size to compete against in timed skirmishes. Standing there against the wall, waiting to see who I was to be paired with, I felt nervous and anxious, and yet those nerves somehow tapped into a part of myself that had thus far been neglected in the womb of my mother's nurture and my foster parents' neglect. The fear reminded me that I was alive, that I was a participant in the world of living things.

It turns out wrestling was a sport I was well-suited for. I secured the third string spot in the 98-pound weight class, which was a good accomplishment for a freshman who had never played sports. This meant I would need to travel with the team to tournaments and matches. The first tournament I participated in, I won three straight matches until I was pinned by our team's own JV wrestler in the final. I was excited beyond words at my modest success. Wrestling would become one of the few consistent parts of my life for years to come. It added positive moments to my disappointing teenage years.

Janice and Lance said they couldn't afford to buy the wrestling shoes I needed, so the coaches had to wrap athletic tape around my ankles to avoid sprains and injuries. Another expense was traveling to the events in other towns, which required money for food when the team would stop to eat. I made a practice of nonchalantly walking in with the team, as though I were going to order food. Then I would grab a handful of crackers or some such appetizer from one of the tables and retreat back to the school bus where I would eat whatever I'd gathered. One of the coaches noticed me sitting on the bus once and asked me why I didn't come in and get some food. Embarrassed, I looked at him and shrugged my shoulders.

"I don't have any money," I honestly replied.

"Do you want me to buy you something?" he asked.

I shook my head. "That's okay, I'm not really hungry." Not wanting to embarrass me further, he looked at me sadly, then turned and went back to the restaurant.

I lasted six months with the Whitmores. Janice's husband, Lance Sr., despised me almost from the beginning as a weak creature. He found it hard not to make disparaging remarks about me, which never failed to secure chuckles from his sons Tony and Jesse. He couldn't resist making unflattering comparisons between me and his son Mitch, with respect to various matters, and though Mitch never encouraged such taunts, he was in no position to stop them either.

"Mitch could whip your ass in no time flat," Lance would proudly declare, as though this were some important piece of information that everyone should take interest in. How do you reply to such commentary? I would simply shrug my shoulders and stare at the floor, waiting for the conversation to change topics.

I could always tell by the frown on Janice's face that she wished they would treat me better, but she too was helpless to intervene. Upon returning from wrestling practice, I was greeted at home by a hostile atmosphere. The vibes reminded me that I lived under their roof only as a guest. I knew not to assume too much about my standing within the household. A lifting of the eyebrows, a sigh, a shake of the head, was all it took to remind me that the food in the fridge was not mine, nor the bed upon which I slept. Their house was not my home. I lived among people who were not my family. Mac fared little better, and spent most of his time outside the house when I was gone, in a constant state of neglect.

One thing Lance Whitmore *was* passionate about in his house was professional wrestling, which he was convinced was absolutely real and un-staged. He watched the wrestling matches with the kind of religious devotion most men his age devoted to college football and the NFL. I too enjoyed watching the shows for entertainment, though I quickly learned better than to say out loud that the whole thing was fixed. Lance took that charge *very* seriously, and it brought out a reaction that warned me to avoid the subject.

So I adopted Rowdy Roddy Piper as my favorite wrestling character, and tried my best to believe it was all real. Lance took great delight in disputing with me about the merits of my choice. He would insult my "hero" with enthusiasm, testing the edges of his limited vocabulary, his eyes wild with a crazy energy. One got the sense that he was taking all of this a bit too seriously. He was a devoted fan of Hulk Hogan, and any exchanges regarding the relative skills of the two combatants could quickly escalate into a tense situation.

During the winter, Lance was frequently off work and was home more often. Janice cleaned houses to help pay the bills. Finances were especially tight at those times, increasing Lance's irritability. Because Mitch and I shared a room, I could not retreat there to find a private haven from the tense atmosphere. So I would walk around the neighborhood alone in the dark, even in the bitter winter evenings. I could always escape into the nurture of the frigid winter nights.

I can still remember the feeling of that cold Oregon air on my face, as I would walk along, heading nowhere, and heading anywhere but the house and its drama. Sometimes groups of laughing teenagers would walk by along the street, cigarettes and beer in their hands, and I would inwardly crave an invitation to join them, while outwardly looking down at the ground and scurrying past without a word.

If the temperatures permitted, I would bring Mac along, and he would silently walk beside me, sniffing with interest at the snow, apparently just as grateful as I was to flee from the tragedy of our sad existence in foster care. Night after night, up and down the streets we would go, walking through school yards, church lawns, parks and city property under the light of the moon and the stars. During daylight hours I would go downtown and hide in the bookstore, where I would thumb through volumes I had no money to buy, until the clerk's attention would pressure me to move on.

At other times I remember walking along snowy roads around the outskirts of town, staring out at the sagebrush, and occasionally noticing with excitement deer and coyote tracks along the road. Anywhere other than the house felt like a garden sanctuary to me. In the open spaces I found room to think and breathe and simply bask in the sunlight of absent-mindedness.

There was a growing sense of restlessness within me. I was always out walking and searching. Maybe deep down inside I was trying to work up the will to take Mac and resolutely head down the road, in an easterly direction, all the way back to Idaho Falls, back to those idyllic sagebrush plains of the Snake River valley where my mother had spent her days. There I could breathe again the air she had breathed, and see again the streets, and the trees, and the distant mountains that had greeted her eyes every day when she limped beside me on this earth. Whatever my intentions, eventually I always found myself back at the front door of the house.

My depression began to creep into other areas of my life. As the winter wore on, I would often skip school, and walk up into the snowy mountains west of town to be by myself. I was greeted by the resident mule deer, whose silent stares from the frozen hillsides helped to calm my soul. I started missing wrestling practice frequently enough to warrant a warning from the assistant coach that I was in danger of being cut from the team. Other 98-pounders would be happy to take my third string slot.

I can't remember imagining anything that I might be one day. I had no dreams or aspirations, or optimism to fuel my hopes. Somewhere in the back of my mind, lay the distant hazy memory of dog shows, but that all seemed like another world given the realities of my situation. Once, I attended the training classes sponsored by a local dog club in La Grande, having seen a flyer announcing their events somewhere, but I soon discovered that I no longer fit in with the dog fancier crowd. Purchasing training equipment, and finding transportation to obedience trials and other events was now well beyond my resources. Standing there by myself in the gymnasium with my ragged and unkempt Miniature Schnauzer, I stood out as a curiosity, like someone who had wandered into the wrong building. I quickly accepted my fate and gave up the effort to belong anywhere.

At Janice's urging, arrangements were made for me to begin speaking with a social worker about my sulking behavior, truancy and depression. It was actually a married couple. They spoke with me about the death of my mother, challenges at school, and the tensions and difficulties of living in the Whitmore home. They seemed very concerned and genuinely compassionate. They were stunned to hear of how seriously professional wrestling was taken in the family and what a source of tension it seemed to be.

In a group session with Lance and Janice present, the male therapist addressed this situation, saying at one point to Lance, "In professional wrestling, the matches are of course fixed. It's purely a show for entertainment. Obviously, we all understand that." Lance looked back at him with a blank expression on his face, saying nothing.

Then one day he just snapped. It was in the backyard, where we were all gathered for some reason. It was a cold, wet day, with grey skies. Maybe we should have been inside, congregating in warm, safe places. Mac was out there too, with Mitch's Chow Chow-mix in the dog pen, and suddenly they started fighting. A Miniature Schnauzer is no match for a Chow Chow, and it was apparent that something had to be done quickly or Mac would be seriously hurt. Mitch and I jumped into the fray and I began to use my foot in the attempt to scare Mitch's dog away, thrusting out with my leg. My kicks were not malicious, or intended to cause harm to Mitch's dog, but only to create enough space between the dogs to enable me to reach down and pull Mac up into my arms.

Finally we got the two separated, and Mitch grabbed his dog and pulled him away. As I walked out of the pen with Mac to carry him to safety, Lance was waiting for me near the back door of the house, a fierce glare etched on his face. I set Mac down and started to walk past him when suddenly he grabbed me by the collar of my coat. He threw me backward in a fit of rage and then lifted me clear off the ground and slammed me against the wall of the house. He let my feet touch the ground and then tossed me back against the wall again. I was shocked at his strength, as he was handling me like a rag doll. He then put his face up close to my own and spat, "I swear to God, if you *ever* touch Mitch's dog again, I will fucking kill you!" I stood still, utterly frozen with fear as he looked hard into my eyes, before he turned his back and walked away.

Of course, Lance was not concerned about *Mitch's dog* at all. This had merely been the flashpoint for the expression of his hostility. He resented my presence in their midst and the space I was taking up in their crappy home. He resented me for being thin and quiet and bookish and weak. He despised me for being the sort of person who would never work in the woods, run a chainsaw or make his way in the world by the sweat of his brow. Clearly I was not designed for that. If I survived at all, it would be by doing things other than the tasks performed by the Lance Whitmores of the world.

Later that week, I divulged what had taken place to my social workers, thinking I was speaking to them in confidence. They promptly reported it to the authorities responsible for child protection, and that brought an end to my sojourn with the Whitmores. I found out within a couple of days that everyone knew I had "told" on Lance, who had suddenly become very quiet at the house. I could see he was avoiding speaking or getting too close to me, probably out of fear that he could not control himself. It was clear that he was furious at me for reporting what had happened to the social workers, yet he also knew now that any further action against me would only bring the attention of the police and cause trouble at the house.

About a week later I was sitting at the kitchen table, pouring some powdered milk over a bowl of cold cereal. Janice came in and poured herself a cup of coffee, then turned and leaned against the counter, facing me, sipping on her drink. She told me that things were just not "working out" with me living there. They had spoken with another half-sister of mine, whom I had never met, named Geraldine. Don and Geraldine Brown lived in Moyock, North Carolina, and they had agreed to let me come and live with them.

"I really think you'll love it out there," she hopefully assured me. The news came as no great surprise. It had long since been clear that I had outstayed my welcome. In fact, I greeted the news of my imminent departure with a measure of relief. I was more than ready to take Mac and get the hell out of there.

When April of my freshman year rolled around, I was again on the move, this time to the other side of the country, to live with the Browns in North Carolina. Lance and Janice Whitmore drove me to Portland.

Without much emotion or fanfare, they put me and Mac on a plane to Washington, D.C. and sent us on our way. The excitement of flying wore off fairly quickly, and I slept most of the way to the nation's capital, where I was to be picked up from the airport. The only thing I really remember about that flight from sea to shining sea was the breakfast meal I was served. The dish of bacon, scrambled eggs and French toast was the most delicious food I could ever remember eating. And I washed it down with a cold glass of real milk.

Arriving in North Carolina (1985)

When I arrived at the airport in D.C. I was nervous. I didn't even know what Don and Geraldine Brown looked like. *Would they like me? Would they let Mac live in the house?* I stepped off the plane and walked into the waiting area where anxious families were gathered to meet arriving loved ones. I could see women with teary eyes embracing their military husbands, and children waving to catch the attention of hard-working fathers returning from long business trips. I stared out into the crowd, and earnestly looked for anyone who appeared as though they might just be looking for me.

Then I saw them. A middle aged couple was standing there with their gaze directed right at me. The woman caught my eye and waved me over. A rush of excitement washed over me as I returned her wave and walked up to them. As I reached them, Geraldine pulled me close to her and hugged me tightly, without even asking my name.

"How was your flight?" she asked.

"It was fine," I said with a lump in my throat, as her husband Don gave me a second hug. He kept his hand on my shoulder in a reassuring way as we briefly chatted about where we would pick up my luggage, including Mac.

Don was a muscular man of medium height and rapidly graying hair, built something like a chimpanzee, with short legs. He was dressed in jeans and a white short-sleeved shirt. Geraldine was a thin woman of medium height, with a tough, deadpan expression. I studied her as we made our way through the airport. She looked like the sort of person who would be there for you in a fight, but who might just as likely be in the fight there with you. I liked both of them immediately.

When we finally got to the area where the traveling animals were transported, Mac was ecstatic to see me, scratching furiously on the door of the crate as I approached. Apart from being very thirsty, and having gone to the bathroom in his crate, he seemed none the worse for wear. Soon my bags and my dog were loaded into their car and we were all on our way. A family. I sat with Mac in the back seat while Don drove and Geraldine engaged me in small talk. The traffic was heavy, and the drivers all around us on the freeway were aggressive in a way which was foreign to me. Driving out of D.C., I felt like I had arrived in a strange new country. I looked out the window while Mac stood on my legs and stared in wonder at our new surroundings.

"Go ahead hero," Don said as he moved to a right lane, allowing some impatient driver to past us. I watched him carefully from the back seat, falling in love. He drove with his left arm hanging outside the window in a casual way, while he calmly steered us through the freeway traffic with his right hand. He was quiet, but not in a haunted or moody way, rather like someone who was not in a rush to speak, but liked to listen and take in a situation. I think he was still trying to size me up before attempting to engage me in much conversation, occasionally glancing at me in the rear view mirror, but I could sense that he already liked me. They both smoked in the car. Geraldine talked to me as we drove while exhaling smoke, slitting her eyes as though studying me during the conversation.

Along the way they told me all about North Carolina, and the two sisters who were awaiting me at home: Elizabeth, age 18, and Eileen, age 13. As we traveled, Don engaged me in conversations about hunting and wildlife, which stirred my hopes and imagination. He told me how he used to hunt deer and elk out in the state of Washington when they lived out there, and promised to take me target shooting with his black powder rifles. He was a firearms expert, having received a lot of weapons training in the Navy and in his years as a police officer. That was all before they had relocated to North Carolina. Now he worked as a professional welder in Norfolk. Geraldine worked as the manager of a convenience store in Currituck County.

It was dark by the time we arrived. The Browns owned a singlewide in the Wedgewood trailer court outside of Moyock. It was a maze of dirt and gravel roads, with rundown trailer homes, defiantly decorated with Confederate flags and old cars in the driveways. The area was surrounded by woods and swamps. I was stirred with excitement as we pulled into the driveway of my new home. *What would the girls think of me? Would they be kind to Mac? Would they introduce me to all their friends?* These and like questions stirred in my mind as we got out of the car and made our way to the front door.

As we walked up the steps with my luggage, my new foster sisters were standing there, waiting to greet me. I walked through the door as Eileen embraced me in a warm hug and said, "Welcome to the family." Her older sister Elizabeth did the same as Eileen took Mac out of my arms and began to cuddle him, declaring with excitement how adorable he was. I studied the scene, as Mac's eyes glowed in the face of all this sudden attention. I sat down on the couch as the two girls began to engage me in non-stop conversation, asking all about where I had lived, what schools I had attended, what my interests and hobbies were, and so forth.

I was shell-shocked that anyone should even care about the trivial details of my life. I was hungry to share, and answered every question they threw at me as the evening wore on. Don and Geraldine sat on the couch in a parental way and watched us break the ice.

Elizabeth was tall and thin, with long, striking red hair that reached down to her waist. She always spoke in a fast and excited tone, balanced with the graces of the incipient maturity that belongs to high school seniors. Eileen was a beautiful girl as well, with developing feminine curves in various stages of adolescence, and medium-length dark hair. She still had hints of her waning childhood, with slight freckles and subtle but noticeable buck teeth. She was very excited about the prospect of starting the ninth grade the following year, and how neat it would be to have a foster brother with her there at the high school, now that "Liz" was graduating. As I sat and basked in the warmth of the attention I was receiving from these talkative girls, it all seemed too good to be true. The Browns weren't rich, but they certainly had the makings of a family that would love and take care of me, and I felt sure I would get along well with these girls.

Then something unexpected happened. Don walked over to the kitchen and pulled two beers out of the fridge, one for him and one for me. He handed it to me without a word, and then walked over to the television. I was fourteen years old. I couldn't believe he had just handed me a beer. I had never been allowed to drink alcohol before in my life. I sipped the beer and held it up, like an archaeologist studying some newly discovered artifact. I locked eyes with Mac, and shrugged at our change of fortunes.

Then Eileen exclaimed, "Oh daddy, you're so gross!" I had no idea what was about to happen. Liz turned to me and said, "Have you ever watched porn before?" I had not, and honestly had no conception of pornography beyond the level of Playboy magazines. A little unsure as to what was transpiring, I stared at the screen.

The movie Don put in had not been rewound, so when the picture materialized, there was no preparatory skit to sit through. On the TV a man and a woman were having sex. My eyes grew to the size of saucers as I looked on. Geraldine and Liz stared at the screen with a bored expression on their faces. Eileen was looking at me to judge my reaction. When I looked over in her direction she rolled her eyes as if to say, "Can you believe *our dad*?" As I sat there on the couch with a beer in my hand and my dog at my feet, taking in my first pornographic movie, the thought suddenly dawned on me that somehow providence was paying me back for all the misery I had endured with the Whitmores and the Huntings. I had finally landed in teenage paradise.

Country Roads (1985-1986)

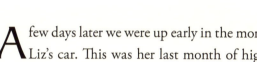

A few days later we were up early in the morning and cramming into Liz's car. This was her last month of high school, and she had a serious case of senioritis. School was no longer a house of learning, but a refuge for nervous teens, seeking courage in numbers as they prepared to leap into the world of adults. Eileen rode with her mother, or took the school bus to the junior high. Along the way, Liz talked to me about all the ins and outs of high school social life. She was a member of the marching band, and a very popular person at school. A central figure among the social elite of Currituck County High. A source of knowledge for all teenage gossip. I felt privileged and intimidated to be with her in the car. I soon learned that she had had several serious boyfriends, but was currently dating an older guy named Bobby, who was in the Navy. Bobby was built like the stereotypical surfer dude. He was muscular and handsome, with blond hair and oozing with quiet boyish charm. Liz's face glowed whenever she mentioned his name.

When we arrived at the high school, there was a period of time in the mornings when everybody was milling about in the cafeteria, sitting on lunch tables or gathered in small groups talking excitedly about the scandals of the weekend.

Doug cheated on Donna!

Amy broke up with Greg!

Andy's dad caught him smoking pot!

And other shocking headlines. Liz marched up to some of her friends and introduced me. However, as a shy, skinny freshman, and brand new to the school at that, I had no chance of breaking into her crowd of sophisticated juniors and seniors. They all offered polite greetings and turned back to their conversations as though I didn't exist. That first morning at least, I was able to hide in their midst until Liz took me to the office and showed me where I needed to register. After that I saw very little of Liz at school.

A month or so passed, and before I knew it, my first high school year mercifully came to an end. Despite attending three different schools as a freshman, I had survived, and had completed enough coursework to progress to my sophomore year. As far as I can recall, I made no friends during that brief period, but neither did I make any enemies. There was no bullying to deal with. The atmosphere at Currituck County High School was much less hostile than the prison yard at La Grande. School fights were rare, and nobody seemed inclined to pick on me or make fun of my appearance.

I spent my lunch hours by myself. I made a habit of sitting down at some isolated table that was either unoccupied or scattered with one or two other misfits. Then I would quickly gulp down my lunch and be on my way. I would go directly outside and walk around the schoolyard, or sit in the sunshine and think. There were always fields to explore out behind the school, and it was easy to pass the span of a lunch break looking for deer tracks along the edge of the woods. It was so much easier to hide than to take the risk of reaching out, joining the dance of teenage society. I preferred the predictability of my own company.

Without realizing it, my experiences had shaped patterns of thought and behavior that would remain with me for the rest of my life. I still feel uncomfortable and vulnerable in groups, and quickly become emotionally drained among people. When surrounded by a crowd, I feel like the world is closing in around me, as though my presence is unwelcome, like an unwanted "party crasher." I feel suddenly conspicuous and lost, as though my very presence is taking up valuable space, and the self-consciousness drains me. I return to the Hunting trailer, or the Whitmore home, desperate to escape to my bedroom, or the chill of the outdoors on a frigid night.

At home, I looked to Don for guidance and fatherly nurturing. He would come home from work early in the afternoons during the summer, and I would follow him around the trailer and the yard in the heat of the sun, studying his every move and mannerism. Like Geraldine, he was a constant smoker, and there was something about the way he handled his cigarettes that commanded my admiration. Somehow, the most mundane of observations are transformed into timeless wisdom when uttered in conjunction with the exhale of cigarette smoke. He was a seemingly endless source of knowledge about women, guns, the outdoors and fighting. Don's range of skills and knowledge seemed particularly crafted to secure my fascination.

In the Navy he had been a boxer, and a very successful one at that, having won some sort of major competition in the military ranks. One hot summer day I was sitting on the couch in our trailer when he emerged from his bedroom with a box. He nonchalantly proceeded to show me his boxing pictures and trophies, as though it were no big deal to him, studying me though, to judge my reaction. He showed me how to throw a punch with a particular curve of the wrist, which would ensure maximum energy delivery on impact. Standing there, trading practice punches on the hands with Don fulfilled some deep longing within me that had been kept at bay my whole life.

Don's account of his boxing exploits spilled over into other stories of violence, as he described some of the things he had occasion to do to people while making arrests as a police officer. He described to me what a wonderful weapon a heavy flashlight can be when busted over a person's skull. Though I sensed all was not right with his stories, I soaked in his machismo and admired him for it. His model of masculinity was all that was offered to me, and I took it.

When it came to women, Don was less than an ideal role model. He had no qualms admitting that he viewed women as intellectually inferior, essentially good for only one thing. As I neared the age of 15, Don assured me he would take me to a local brothel, where I could experience the love of a real woman.

And yet, despite Don's crude attitudes toward the opposite sex, it was clear that women found him somehow charming. As a young man he had been a tough and handsome playboy, and many women had seemed to find his coarse manner alluring. It was plain that Geraldine was madly in love with him, and Eileen adored him as though he were the model father. Even Eileen's young friends seemed to find his perverseness somehow endearing, perhaps because he had a knack for being so blatantly shameless about it. When Eileen would walk through the front door with one of her friends, Don would remark as they walked by with his particular brand of wit.

"My oh my, you are growin' one *nice* set of titties!"

Or perhaps with equal charm. "Mmm! You have got one *fine* ass!"

Eileen would roll her eyes, her friends would blush and giggle, and then the girls would scamper off into the bedroom or back outside.

Don was an avid black powder shooter. He owned two rifles (a .54 and a .58 caliber), and a black powder pistol just like the weapons used in the movie *The Good, the Bad and the Ugly*. On Saturdays, he would sometimes take me down to the county dump, where we would climb out of his rickety old blue pickup truck, unload all our trash, and then fire off the guns for a while.

The pistol was especially fun to shoot. It made a satisfying "clunking" sound as it went off, and the recoil made you feel peculiarly alive in that brief moment after pulling the trigger. Loading and firing black powder weapons is a unique experience with a particular nostalgia. Shooting those primitive guns made me feel connected to my romantic image of the distant past, when not so long ago men of nerve and determination traveled west and explored the mysteries of the Rocky Mountains, braving their winter storms and other dangers with an admirable masculine impunity.

I was so desperate to go deer hunting. I sat with earnest attention as Don would describe his past hunting exploits to me. He promised that when fall rolled around, he and I would venture out into the nearby swamps, set up a deer stand and spend the dawns and dusks out in the woods, hunting the elusive Whitetail. I lusted over hunting gear and equipment in catalogues I picked up from various places. I studied everything I could get hold of to teach me about black powder weapons, and the hunting techniques particular to eastern Whitetails.

I daydreamed about deer hunting constantly. I imagined getting up with Don in the darkness of early morning. Silently we would make our way out of the trailer into the chilly air. The women would still be sound asleep of course, oblivious to our manly adventures. We would get into his pickup and quietly shut the doors, to avoid making undue noise. Then we would back out of the driveway and head to our chosen spot. Together we would walk into the woods and take our stations in the deer stand until a mature buck ventured across our path. Breathless at the sight of the beautiful creature, but resolute in the task of filling my deer tag and securing meat and a trophy, I would carefully take aim. Soon, we are down on the ground, and Don is patting me on the back, shaking my hand and congratulating me on making such a fine shot, proud of my kill just as though he had calmly bagged the trophy himself.

Well, by the time my sophomore year rolled around, Don had begun to take welding jobs which paid lucrative wages, but took him far from home, to locations in Wyoming and West Virginia. I spoke with him on the phone several times, and always brought up the topic of our planned deer hunting trip. He continued to promise me that we would go out before the season ended, but that fall came and went, and I gradually realized Don's words counted for very little, whatever his intentions might have been.

As the school year got underway, I saw less and less of Don. I drew more deeply inward, hiding from the world within myself. Outwardly I might have seemed to fit in okay, though maybe a bit of a loner. I tried out for the wrestling team, and this time secured the Varsity spot at the 112-pound weight class. I enjoyed modest success that season, winning half of my matches and qualifying for the sectional first stage toward the state finals. The Browns at least provided me with wrestling shoes, and money for food on my trips, though they usually didn't attend my matches. Don was out of the state, and Geraldine spent her evenings playing Bingo at the town hall, or drinking wine coolers in front of the TV in her bathrobe in our trailer.

Around this time I met what I guess I would call my first girlfriend in high school. As it turned out, she would also be my last until college. Her name was Beth Walker. She was a thin, lanky blond with a shy personality, a close friend of Eileen's. We were first introduced in front of a convenience store, where for some reason Geraldine had arranged to pick up Eileen, and I was along for the ride. Eileen came over to the car and told me she wanted me to meet her friend Beth, that Beth thought I was "cute." Flattered, I looked out the window (trying to look cool) as Eileen then went inside and reappeared at the door, dragging her mortified friend by the arm behind her. Beth was giggling as fourteen-year-old girls do, covering her face and trying desperately to get back into the safety of the store. She never said hi that day, but I got my first glimpse of her. The notion that this pretty blond with her long legs had an interest in me made my heart beat a little faster.

A few days later, Beth invited me and Eileen over to her house. She lived in a trailer on the outskirts of Wedgewood. When we came in the door Beth introduced me to her strikingly beautiful mother. I instantly fell in love with that kind woman, and the warm greeting I received from her brought me back to my experiences with Pam and her mom. Despite my ragged appearance, and my obvious place on the social scale as a fellow-resident of Wedgewood, Beth's mother seemed to sense something in me that put her at ease. Though I had all the normal hormones of a teenage boy, she could tell that I was unlikely to plunge her daughter into ruin.

From that day on, for some time to come, our visits to Beth's house became fairly frequent, and she spent a lot of time over at our trailer as well. We kissed, and explored each other, fumbling our way through our time in the trailer court. Neither of us was old enough to drive, and we lacked both the money and the parental supervision that might have enabled us to go out and do constructive, positive things together.

But despite having a girlfriend and casual friendships on the wrestling team, inwardly I was getting more and more lost. Don's frequent absences left me feeling abandoned, as so many of my hopes and aspirations were tied up with him. My thoughts increasingly drifted back to Idaho. Oh how I longed to return to the land of my origins. Idaho seemed so distant now, that it might as well have been on another planet. I daydreamed about the sagebrush and the mountains during my classes. I spent many lunch periods in the library, looking up Idaho in the Encyclopedia, staring at the pictures, wondering if my eyes had ever gazed at those very spots, and memorizing the statistics of populations, economy and agriculture. I wrote out lists of all the main cities in Idaho,

Wyoming, and Montana, and ranked them in order in terms of my preference as a place to live once I grew up.

At home I became increasingly antisocial and isolated. Eileen and I grew distant from one another, as upon returning home from school my most immediate course of action was to barricade myself in my bedroom. Sometimes, sensing my depression, Geraldine or Eileen would knock on the door and ask if I wanted to come out in the living room and watch TV. I would decline with a gloomy reply, and the door would close again. Things became tense in the house, and Eileen's overtures of friendship soon turned to hostility. I didn't belong there. As the months wore on we bickered more and more frequently.

I had few avenues of escape from the trailer. On Saturdays I worked for a wealthy old man who owned a beautiful plot of land just west of Wedgewood. It had a pond and scenic surroundings, enclosed by cornfields and patches of woodland. He planned to retire in a few years and intended to build a home on this reclusive property. Another boy my age and I were hired to help him clear the land and build fences around the property. We were paid $2 an hour, plus lunch; even at that time it seemed like pretty cheap labor.

He spoke to us often as we worked, about Labradors, duck hunting, women and the mysteries of life, but he was too old to serve as much of a father figure. The only quote of his that sticks in my memory was a statement he made to the boy I worked with, regarding the fondness the man and I shared for chewing tobacco.

"That's right," he gravely told him once while we were driving in his van along some country lane. "We ain't pussies. We chew tobacco." The boy quietly considered that commentary on the nature of manhood, but it did not seem to shift his opinion that it was a disgusting habit.

Mostly, when I was not at wrestling practice or working, I was wandering. Whereas in Oregon my memory is dominated by images of wandering at night in the winter, in North Carolina I am ever wandering in the heat of the summer during the day. Up and down the lonely country roads I would walk, wandering aimlessly, surveying the canals, fields and swamps around me. I was always staring at the edges of the woods, looking for deer. Sometimes I would venture out across the fields to the tree line and look for tracks, which I inevitably found, though I did not see the elusive Whitetail the whole time I was there. My failure to see them increased their mystery, giving them an almost supernatural character. Like God, they could not be seen directly, though the signs of their presence were everywhere if I would only go and look.

I really hated the flat landscape around me, mostly because it was not Idaho. Yet at the same time, the swamps held a strange allure, and drew me often into their bosom. There I would wander the game trails, studying the foliage, looking for deer sign, listening to the crickets and the squirrels and the birds, wondering about the black bears and bobcats which I knew were there with me behind the veil of the leaves. I found a certain solace in the quietness of the trees, and hid there for lengthy stretches, until nervousness about snakes and the torture of the mosquitoes became too much to take.

All this time, Mac was there with me, silently suffering, faithful at all times. He was horribly infested with fleas and ticks during the warm summer months, and though I did my best to help him, we were outnumbered, and without access to veterinary care. I battled the parasites beside him, enduring nearly constant fleabites in my dirty bedroom, and pulling ticks out of my own body almost as often as his. I had a small mark on my skin for years from a tick that I removed improperly, leaving its head embedded within me as a reminder of my stay in Currituck County. Despite the conditions we lived in, Mac never ceased his daily ritual of dancing a jig upon my every return to our cluttered trailer. It is not within the nature of a dog to question providence.

There was a particular pond near our trailer court that I would often retreat to in those days, and sit there for hours pondering my life, missing my mother and trying to peer into my future.

Where was I going to go from here?

I knew somehow that this could not be my final destination, but the way forward seemed obscure and impossible to discern. I heard a John Denver song playing on the radio once, on a ride home after a day's work picking fruit on a local farm for spending money. Its lyrics touched my heart in a way I will never forget, and I began to sing it to myself during my restless walks.

"Country roads, take me home, to the place I belong. West Virginia, mountain mama, take me home, country roads." That song became my daily prayer in my wandering seclusion and, as events turned out, somebody was listening.

Broken Promises (1986)

"We are getting a divorce."

She said it calmly, while sitting next to Don on the couch, smoking a cigarette as she always did, with his arm draped around her. I could scarcely believe my ears. Don had returned from one of his trips, and announced that he and Geraldine had something they needed to tell us. Curious as to what this might be, I sat with rapt attention in the living room. *Were we moving? Adopting another child? Buying a house?*

Divorce was the last thing I expected of Don and Geraldine, who always seemed deeply affectionate, playful and passionately in love with one another. If anything, their constant sexual frivolity was embarrassing. Sure they argued and fought from time to time, but nobody would have expected them to go their separate ways.

"Why?" I asked, in shock.

"Because Don says I've been cheating on him, and I haven't," she calmly replied, extinguishing a cigarette in the ashtray. I looked at Don and he raised his eyebrows with a slight nod of affirmation.

What struck me as peculiar was the lack of emotion in the room.

Here was a married couple who had built up years of memories together and shared their lives in the most intimate of ways, and yet their imminent split was announced as though they were speaking of changing the carpet in the living room.

"We've decided green carpet would look better. Oh, and we're divorcing, so that we can live separate lives from now on. By the way, is there any beer left in the fridge?"

I looked at Eileen, and could tell by the expression on her face that she already knew about this. As the foster kid, I was of course out of the loop and the last to be informed.

With hindsight, the end of Don and Geraldine's marriage shouldn't have come as any great surprise. This was a deeply dysfunctional family. The trailer was awash with pornography, despite the presence of children. Next to the TV were stacks of porn videos, which we could watch at any time, and magazines like *Penthouse* and *Hustler* were scattered about the place, much like one might find copies of *Good Housekeeping* and *TV Guide* lying around a typical house. Pornography was regarded as normal viewing for any person at the age of puberty or above. The conversations around the trailer were often charged with inappropriate sexual content toward the girls.

I remember one day I came home to a chaotic scene. I was told that Liz was being kicked out of the house, and Eileen and I were charged with the task of tossing her belongings out in the yard. Eileen and Liz were not getting along well at that time, so she was more than willing to carry out her assigned duty. I, however, was faced with a moral conundrum. Liz had always treated me well, and had never given me any reason to dislike her. But, I was desperate to prove my loyalty to Don.

So I helped Eileen toss Liz's clothes, books and other belongings out onto the grass in front of our sad old trailer. Carrying boxes in my arms, I repeatedly opened up the rickety front door screen. Standing on the front steps I was met time and again by our dirt driveway and the rundown trailers across the cul-de-sac from us. This is the view that had greeted Liz every morning when leaving for school, carrying her books in her arms, dressed to fit in with her peers. And now her childhood was ending with an unceremonious eviction.

The reason for this sudden turn of events was initially obscure. It supposedly had something to do with promiscuous behavior on Liz's part. But when Don and I were alone in the trailer, he confessed that he had said something to Liz.

"I told her if she was going to put out for every boy in the county, she might as well pay her rent by putting out here." Don had told Liz that she must now give out sexual favors, or leave. When she refused, he told her to pack up her things and get out. He of course denied that he had ever said this to her, as it would not have sat well with Geraldine and Eileen. But he seemed to feel it was safe to make me privy to the information. I had no idea how to respond to his confession; by this point I had lost all hope of figuring out what normal family behavior was supposed to look like.

Geraldine had struggled to hold the family together. She did her best to get close to me, but our relationship was hard to define. She was my biological half-sister, but precisely the age of a mother. She had no idea what to do about my depression and isolation. I spent most of my time in my room. When she was home she was exhausted from work, and sat in front of the TV sipping on wine coolers and chain smoking. Neither of us was inclined to engage in much conversation.

There were a few occasions though, when the veil came down, and wordless connections managed to penetrate our dysfunctional relationship. Usually this would happen in the car. I still feel strangely warmed when I recall trips to the store together, or errands to various places. The weather is warm and humid, and I am again sitting there beside her in the passenger seat with Mac in my lap, the window open, just thankful

119

that Geraldine has allowed us to come along. We engage in small talk, but mostly I just stare out the window as lonely swamps and green fields pass before my eyes, while she drags on her cigarette beside me.

There was in those moments a quiet understanding. Having escaped from the tense atmosphere of the trailer, I found myself attached to her, with her quiet, broody manner. She was not a surrogate mother; but the bond which tied us to our father's history was palpable, and created an affection which all too rarely had the chance to come to the surface. I grasped, by some kind of latent instinct, the meaning of her selective communication, and her piercing glances. Buried within her was a shared storyline, stretching back through the generations, which formed the backdrop to her origin and mine; and it made me love her without being able to explain why that was exactly.

On those trips we would always stop somewhere, and she would buy me a soft drink, which made the short ride feel like a mini-vacation. I was free, at least for a little while, from the fleas and the boredom and the hopelessness of our pornography-drenched trailer; free from agonizing over their neglected black dog who was always tied up and ignored in the back yard; free from the tired streets and run-down cul-de-sacs of Wedgewood; free from the depressing spectacle of daytime programs like *Ricky Lake*, *Oprah* and *Montel Williams*, which were always playing on the TV.

Once Don and Geraldine announced their divorce though, I was put in the difficult position of choosing between them. Would I stay with my half-sister Geraldine, or eventually go to live with Don? In the spring of my sophomore year, everything in that little trailer began to fall apart. Don was working in West Virginia (where it turns out he was deeply involved with another woman, who years later would be the cause of his untimely death), traveling back and forth periodically to see the family, but tensions ran high. Eileen's loyalty shifted to her mother, and Liz's boyfriend Bobby was threatening to do Don bodily harm. I was the only one left standing, uneasily, on Don's side. I had waited 15 years for a father, and was not eager to give this one up, no matter how deeply flawed he might be.

Then one night I received a phone call. Ruth Hudson was on the line. Somehow she had heard about all that was taking place, and the decision had been made that I was to return to Idaho. Tickets had been purchased, and I would be leaving . . . tomorrow. Though the thought of returning to Idaho excited me, I was shocked at the suddenness of it all. There were people at school, kids from the wrestling team, my coach. I would never get the chance to say goodbye to them, not to mention Geraldine, Eileen and Liz. I was simply to vanish, as though my tenure in North Carolina had all been a dream.

And then, suddenly, my thoughts turned to their black Labrador-mix, quietly sitting out there in the back yard. Ever alone, tail wagging upon any hint of attention. Sentenced to solitary confinement in the heat of the sun and fury of the rain, for the crime of existence. Though he wasn't allowed to stay in the house, I had always done my best to make sure he was watered and fed, and received some attention. He greeted me with warm eyes when I ventured out the back door.

Now, with my sudden departure, I was overwhelmed with a sense of guilt at my inability to protect him. I began to sob uncontrollably, and explained my fears about the dog to Don. He looked at me, clearly puzzled that in the midst of all of this, my primary concern was over the care of their backyard dog. But he promised to make sure the dog was looked after, with enough feigned sincerity to put an end to my sobbing and sudden hysteria. That dog haunts me to this day. To me, he embodies all that is broken and wrong with this world.

The next morning we got up very early and drove to Norfolk, where Don took me and Mac to catch a plane to Salt Lake City. Geraldine and Eileen had been staying somewhere else while Don was there at the trailer, and had no idea what was transpiring that morning.

I can still remember standing there with Don in the waiting area of the airport until the time came for me to board my flight.

"You take care of yourself," he said. His face looked sad.

"I will," I replied as he gave me a final hug. In that moment I looked into his soul. "When you go out to Wyoming again on your next welding job, do you *promise* you will come and see me?"

"Absolutely," he lied. I turned my back and walked onto my flight, knowing I would never see Don Brown again.

Ruth Hudson (1986)

My flight from Norfolk made a connection in Atlanta, and then made its way to Salt Lake City. During one leg of the trip, I sat next to a friendly man who struck up a conversation with me. He was middle-aged, with a thick brown mustache. He told me he traveled around the country with a "Christian comedy" group. Seeing that I was traveling alone, he inquired why I was moving by myself from North Carolina all the way back to Idaho.

Since we had plenty of time on our hands, I told him my whole story. He sat quietly and listened as I explained how several years ago my mother had died, leaving me to the care of an aunt and uncle. Then they got tired of me living with them and sent me to live with some relatives in Oregon. That lasted about six months, then I was sent to live with some other relatives in North Carolina. I was with them for about a year, but then they got divorced, so now I was headed back to Idaho where I started.

He looked at me with sad eyes as I shared my story, saying very little, only interjecting short questions and comments now and then.

As we were nearing our destination though, he turned to me. "It sounds like you have had a hard time of it lately. I wish there was something I could say or do for you. I just want you to know that even if it seems sometimes that people don't care about you the way that they should, God does. God sees and he cares."

I sat for a minute and took that in, his directness throwing me off guard. Pondering his words, I stared out the window as we were landing. I could think of nothing to say in reply to that, so I remained quiet until we left our seats and went our separate ways.

I had never been a particularly religious person, even though I was blessed and baptized as a child in the Church of Jesus Christ of Latter-day Saints. Somehow its way of looking at the world never took root in my soul, maybe because my mother was pretty ambivalent about the Mormon religion. Prior to her death, I had attended church on Sundays, but I always felt out of place. Most children attended church with their own families, but I was always seated with some other family or group of children. I felt like a visitor, who just never quite fit in.

I never understood what was happening during their mysterious "sacrament meetings," and was bored most of the time. Now and then, the topic of going on a "mission" would come up in Sunday school, but I never expected to go on a mission when I turned nineteen. How would my mother ever afford something like that? Not planning to go on a mission (as young LDS men are expected to do), not having my imagination fueled by that dream, contributed toward my ambivalence. In reality, the Mormon Church was a spiritual foster family for me. I knew that I would never find a home among them.

Despite my lack of church involvement at the time, when the kind man on the plane told me that God "cared" for me, I didn't doubt him. But neither did it do me much good. A caring God, who sympathized with my suffering, and agonized over my mistreatment, was not what I needed at the time. What I needed was *a saving God*, a God who would take control of the course of my story and point it in a positive direction. Such a God, if he existed, had thus far been absent from my experience. It seemed as though this "caring" God would continue to stand there and pathetically empathize with me.

When I finally landed in Salt Lake City, I distinctly remember studying the pictures on the walls of the airport as I walked through the crowds toward the luggage area. Scenes of mountains, city lights at night, and other pleasant scenes greeted my arrival. I had no idea who would be picking me up. Waiting for me at the airport, was none other than Jean Pugh. She had been appointed by Ruth to drive down and get me, thus avoiding the costs involved in a direct flight to Idaho Falls. On the way up to Idaho Falls we stopped at a truck-stop restaurant and I enjoyed a delicious cheeseburger, smothered in ketchup and mushrooms. All in all, it was a good day.

Now that I was back, it had to be decided where I should live. Returning to live with Norman and Bonnie was not an option. Aunt Marie and Uncle Howard were now living in Loveland, Colorado, and the condo they were in did not allow children. None of my other relatives was offering to take me, so it was decided that I would move in with Ruth, who was now in her mid-sixties. Her husband had passed away a few years earlier, and she lived alone in a nice house with her Shih Tzu as a companion. Her house was only a couple of blocks from where my mother and I had last lived together. There was plenty of room for me and Mac in Ruth's spacious home, so the arrangement seemed sensible. I promptly registered at Idaho Falls High School, and began to make a few friends on the wrestling team (freestyle season was now in full swing).

The situation had potential. I can remember walking to school a few days after I arrived. Though it was early May, snow had fallen on the mountains to the east of town, and all around me the air was crisp and alive. I was thankful to be back on Idaho soil. For awhile it made me feel at home, and things were going well for me at school. I was hanging around with kids from the wrestling team, sitting with them at lunchtime and assemblies. I even reconnected with Richard and Betty Moore and took Mac for visits to see their Airedale Brandy.

Ruth Hudson was a devout Roman Catholic who attended Mass faithfully every Sunday, always inviting me to come along. I spent my Sunday mornings reading and wandering reverently around the quiet spaces within her home. Alone in the house, I drew comfort listening to the rhythm of the steady click emitting from her clock on the living room wall. I had not darkened the halls of any church building for several years now, not since that ill-fated visit to the Lutheran church with my mother. I had no intentions of getting religious any time soon. I worshipped solitude and quiet places.

Living with Ruth did not work out. I lasted a few strained months with her. By this time, with all the experiences I had accumulated over the last few years, I had developed patterns of thinking and behavior that Ruth had no way of anticipating. I was prone to depression and isolation, and when I came home from school or wrestling practice, my instinct was to take Mac and hide myself away in my room with a stack of books.

Ruth could not understand why I would not want to be more sociable. Her attempts to draw me out into the living room, to eat ice cream and watch *Wheel of Fortune*, *Matlock* and her other favorite TV programs, created a tension between us which naturally caused offense. I perceived her as a nosy old busy-body, who was unwilling to give me space and allow me time to myself, and she perceived me as a rude, anti-social, truculent teenager who needed to be more thankful for the roof over his head. She was right mostly, but getting me from where I was, to where I needed to be, was not something within her capacity.

Being once again in the care of a single-parent, and a woman at that, had a strange effect on me. I was back where I had started with my mother. Norman, Lance and Don were hardly good role models, but at least they had played the part. Now I was once again in the position of being raised by a woman, with no role model in the home to show me how to become a man.

When I was not hiding in my room, I returned to my natural urge to roam. A boy at fifteen wants to begin to assert himself and spread his wings. Increasingly I wanted to be out and about with my friends Kevin Aoki and Matt Storm. I was getting especially close to Kevin, who came from a wealthy Japanese family, and whose friendship I found flattering. He was a big deal at high school, and an extremely accomplished wrestler, ranked in the top 5 in the nation at his weight class.

Kevin's family seemed to like me, and I began to spend a lot of time in their home, often joining them for supper. I would sit there with them at the dinner table, listening to the banter, passing the salt, pouring myself a glass of milk. Kevin enjoyed so many of the things that I wished for in my own life, but knew I would never have. For her part, Ruth resented my increasingly frequent periods of absence from the house, and worried that I might be getting into trouble. She had no way of knowing that drugs, alcohol and crime were far from our minds. The more she questioned me and attempted to curtail my outings with Kevin, the more I grew to resent her meddling in my social life. Inevitably it all came to a head.

One evening in early summer I announced my plans to go out and drive around with Kevin. She told me I had been out enough that week, and that there were some chores at the house I had yet to accomplish. She was right, but given the context of our tensions, I felt like she just wanted to keep me from socializing with my friends. In my frustration I called Kevin back, with Ruth standing there, and told him to go ahead and come get me anyway. Ruth warned me that if I left the house I would not have a home to come back to, but I ignored her, assuming it was an idle threat.

Surely she wouldn't kick me out of the house over such a trivial matter, I assured myself. Kevin arrived in his car and swooped me away.

We drove around town for a while, drinking Coke and winking at girls in adjacent cars at stoplights, then parked behind the public library. As the sun was setting and the air beginning to cool, we sat on the hood of his car and began to talk. I complained about Ruth's unreasonable rules at the house, like requiring me to buy my own clothes and personal items. As the evening wore on, I eventually had to stop complaining and go home. When Kevin dropped me off, I found a police car waiting for me outside the house.

I had finally reached the end of the road. I expected to be handcuffed and taken away to jail. The policeman at the house told me he had already spoken to Ruth, and asked me for my side of the story, so I explained to him the whole situation. When I had finished he said, "You know what I think?" "No, what?" I replied, wiping tears from my cheeks. "I think you are a spoiled little punk, and you should be grateful that she's been putting up with your bullshit for all this time. If you were my son I'd bend you over my knee and whip your ass."

Hearing the policeman tell me I was "spoiled" didn't sit well with me. "You don't know anything about me," I said to him with a cool glare, not caring at this point what he was going to do with me. I was ready to get into the police car and go to jail.

"Well, pack up some of your things," he said. "You're not staying here any more." By this time Ruth had joined us out in the front yard. "Do you have any friends you could stay with? Cause if not, I'll have to take you down and get you checked in at Harbor House."

I thought of Kevin, but before I could say anything, Ruth intervened.

"No officer, I don't think that would be a good idea. Just take him to Harbor House." Harbor House was a group home for teenage children who were wards of the state.

"What about Mac?" I asked, feeling a sudden panic.

"He can stay here with me," she curtly replied.

All the fight in me was gone by now, so rather than argue the point, I just walked into the house, pulled out my old military duffel bag which Don Brown had given me, and stuffed it full of clothes. Mac lay on the floor, watching me, sensing the hopelessness of my demeanor. I sat down with him and buried my face in his soft fur. Sobbing in frustration, I explained to him that I was going to be staying somewhere else for awhile, and I wished I could take him with me, but it just wasn't possible.

"You're such a good dog," I assured him, looking into his trusting brown eyes as he looked back at me, panting. "Ruth will take good care of you. When I get things sorted, I'll come and get you." With that, I kissed him on the head, and left the house. I walked past Ruth without a word, and climbed into the back of the police car.

Harbor House (1986)

That evening, the policeman drove me to another part of town, the same neighborhood where I had lived in the second and third grade in fact, only a block from Christian's dad. I knew both what and where Harbor House was. I had often walked by there and seen kids of various ages and sizes sitting on the porch, or raking leaves in the front yard. I always had this vague idea that it was a place where "bad kids" went, who had somehow managed to get themselves into trouble. And now I was sitting in a police car, pulling up to that very location. There was a cement pathway leading up from the sidewalk to the front of the house. We ascended the wooden steps of the porch and knocked on the front door. The porch light was on, and we stood there awkwardly, as moths fluttered around us, and crickets talked in the distance.

The door opened, and we were greeted by the middle-aged couple in charge of the facility. The woman was short and heavy set. The man was tall, with very black hair, a black beard and mustache. He looked like a pirate, minus the earring and scarf. He was not fat, but was solidly built, and had an imposing presence. Teenage boys would not be tempted to challenge him.

After some formalities, the policeman left, and I sat in the TV room, chatting nervously with the house parents and taking in my new surroundings. There was a dining room across from me, and behind that the kitchen area. Off to my left was the downstairs bathroom. As I sat there and talked, the other occupants made brief appearances. At that time, there were only three of us staying there, me and two teenage girls. One of the girls was a shy, plump brunette, the other was a stunning redhead with long legs and a streetwise demeanor. Neither of them spoke to me, though they glanced in my direction out of curiosity as they made their way past.

The woman escorted me up the old stairway to my small room. It was humble, but clean and comfortable. The rules were explained to me. I had to be up and out of the house by 9 a.m. Each morning my room had to be clean and my bed made. There was a schedule with assigned chores that I was responsible for, and they were not negotiable. I had to be home by 6 p.m. to report in and eat supper, and I had to be in the house by 10 p.m. for the evening. What I did from 9 a.m. to 6 p.m. was up to me, but I was not allowed to hang around the house.

The woman was polite, but not overly friendly as she spoke with me. The man I found to have a gruff demeanor, though he got my attention when I found out a few days later that he was an avid bow hunter. He had traveled all over the United States hunting big game. I was impressed, though there was something about the man that kept me at arm's length and prevented me from warming to him too much.

That first evening, after speaking with me for a bit, the woman left me in my room and closed the door behind her. I sat there in the stillness of my solitude and contemplated where life had taken me. I had nothing in this world but the clothes in my bag. Everything else had been taken away from me. My dog, my childhood books and my family pictures were all now in the care of Ruth Hudson.

Where was I going to go from here?

Who was going to help me now?

I was stunned by my lack of options. There was no one I could turn to for guidance and advice. I could not think of any adult who still cared what I was turning out to be. I was the black sheep of the family. That evening, and throughout my stay at Harbor House, I missed my mother more than ever before. I was truly and completely abandoned.

I spent my days and evenings running around with Kevin that summer, pretending that my lack of a family was of no consequence. We would go out to Rigby Lake and sit by the shore looking for girls to chat with, or drive around in the desert, or explore the nearby mountains. In the evenings we could be found in Kevin's car, wandering without purpose around the streets of Idaho Falls, energized by the vitality of our youth. I was only at Harbor House when I had to be there for required residence hours or the completion of assigned chores.

My fleeting attempts to charm the beautiful redhead at the house came to nothing, despite Kevin's "expert" advice. It turns out she was 16, but dating some local man in his twenties that I discerned it would be best to steer clear of. She claimed to have been living on her own since she was thirteen, sometimes sleeping on the streets, and I had no cause to doubt her. Her father was abusive, and she had eventually flown from the pain of her home to try her wings in the world.

The heavy brunette was shy and awkward. Like me, she was basically a decent kid, rarely getting into much trouble, mainly living at Harbor House because of delinquent parenting. Her upbringing had taken her self-esteem, but it hadn't taken her quiet manner and harmless nature. Whereas the redheaded beauty inspired my attraction, this girl inspired my sympathy. Like me, they were both broken teens who needed somebody to offer a helping hand. I hope somebody did.

I maintained a cordial, if cool, relationship with the "parents" of the home during my stay there. The man drafted me into his service, helping him build a shed on some property he had purchased out in the country near Rigby. He informed me that these sorts of tasks were part of my obligatory household chores. For several days we toiled away, laying the foundation, and then building the walls and roof of the small structure. I found that kind of work dull and tortuous, and was paid nothing for my labors. He did buy me lunch at least, rewarding me with stories about his exotic hunting trips.

Though I knew next to nothing about construction and carpentry, I got the sense that he was building this shed "on the cheap," and taking shortcuts on its construction. Somehow that made the task even more annoying. He struck me as the sort of person who did everything as cheaply and quickly as possible, ever desiring more out of life than providence had allotted him.

My experience at Harbor House taught me lessons. It taught me how vulnerable we are in this world, how subject we are to the unpredictable course of fate. How affected we are by the free choices of others. Growing up, I had never anticipated being a teenager, utterly alone in the vastness of the busy world. But that was precisely the situation where I now found myself. I had access to a phone at Harbor House, but who was I going to call?

I no longer mattered.

Boy Meets God (1986)

One morning in July I came downstairs and was told by the house mother that I had two potential foster families to live with. One was a social worker who had been become aware of my case. I was familiar with him from my former life, as he had been a casual acquaintance of Terry and my mother. We used to attend a monthly meal that was held downtown, which was aimed at helping poor families, and he was one of the social workers who attended the meals. Terry told me that he was gay, but I had never thought much of it. Now here he was offering me a place to live.

However, he was not my only option. A woman was also going to be stopping by that afternoon to meet me. Her name was Bonnie Lockes. She and her husband Jim had a good track record dealing with at-risk teens, and the social welfare authorities had contacted her about me.

Later that day, both potential foster parents arrived on my doorstep, around the same time. The man arrived first. He was a tall, thin, clean-shaven man with a balding head. He had a friendly demeanor, but I felt a little uneasy about taking him up on his offer of a home. On the eve of turning 16, the prospect of living alone with a single gay man was a bit off-putting. We sat in the TV room and chatted for a few minutes, as he reminded me of some of his memories of my mother. Though he was not an ideal "family," he was affable enough to make me consider whether it might be an improvement on my situation at Harbor House.

And then Bonnie Lockes arrived. A short, flat-chested, red-haired woman, dressed in a ranch-style shirt and tight blue jeans was knocking on the door. The house mother greeted her and invited her in. She walked up to me and said, "I take it you must be Paul then."

I stood there awkwardly and nodded. She closed the distance between us and, without a word, pulled me to her, holding me tight in a close embrace. I stood stiff at first, but felt my shoulders begin to relax as she rubbed my back with her palms. After what seemed like a long time, she let me go. I could see that she had tears in her eyes as she began to make small talk with the other people in the room. Mostly she talked about the ranch in Leadore where she and her family lived. Now and then she would mix in religious references.

"Praise the Lord. . . . I give all the glory to God. . . . Well Jesus has never let us down."

Finally she turned back to me. She explained that in a few days she was going to be serving as a cook for a group of boys camping out in the wilderness near Stanley, Idaho.

"Why don't you come with us and see how you like it? Then you can decide what you want to do from there."

It was a little uncomfortable for me, as the other man was standing right there, also offering me a home, and I felt like they were bidding for me at a market or something. I distinctly remember Bonnie mentioning that they had a Great Pyrenees who guarded the sheep on their ranch. The potential foster dad replied, "I've got a great pair a knees," while shaking his legs back and forth. Bonnie looked on, clearly wanting me not to go live with him without giving it more thought.

What could it hurt to go on a camping trip for a week or so anyways?

I looked at the man and said, "I think maybe I'll go with her."

"Well then, go get your stuff," she ordered, while giving her hands a clap and rubbing them together.

The next thing I knew, I was getting into a beat up old blue car parked in front of Harbor House. There were two other people in the car; a dark-haired woman, whose face was so eerily similar to my mother that I was taken aback at first, and her teenage son, whom I immediately recognized. His name was Pete, and he had been in the same class with me in the second and third grades in Idaho Falls. Now they lived in Leadore, where his mother ran the general store. They were in town to do some shopping at K-Mart, and Bonnie had caught a ride with them into Idaho Falls. Pete was just as I had remembered him in childhood; quiet, effeminate, bookish, dirty. It seems there was reluctance on the part of that family to do much bathing, and I was always struck by Pete's body odor and greasy, blond hair. He now had glasses, and was tall and thin, but otherwise much the same. Together we made our way across town to the K-Mart parking lot, where Pete and his mom went in to buy some things. I stayed out in the car with Bonnie.

I sat quietly as Bonnie offered a few bits of small talk, and then she suddenly changed the topic of conversation.

"So what about Jesus Christ? Do you know him?"

I looked at her blankly, and shrugged my shoulders.

"Have you accepted him as your personal Lord and Savior?"

I looked in the direction of the K-Mart building, wondering how long Pete and his mom would be.

Not sure how to answer, I offered, "I was raised Mormon, but I don't go to church anymore."

"I'm not asking you whether you go *to church*," she countered, staring directly at me. "I'm asking if you *know* Jesus Christ, personally. I mean *really* know him." She was squeezing her fists for emphasis as she said this. I was not at all sure how I should answer her question. I didn't want to say *no*, lest she take a dislike to me. But I didn't want to say *yes* either, and eventually be found out a liar.

All I could honestly say was, "I don't know. I guess I'm not sure."

Bonnie studied me. "That's okay," she said. "Maybe on this camping trip you'll find out, huh?" She then offered me a tight-lipped, but reassuring smile. I breathed a sigh of relief as she started speaking again about her family and the ranch they lived on.

Bonnie and her husband Jim had two children. Their daughter Tina was my age, and they also had a son Troy who was serving in the military. They raised sheep and cattle on a spacious ranch in Leadore, about two hours north of Idaho Falls. I was intrigued by the location, as it became clear that the area was saturated with wildlife. Mule deer, antelope, coyotes, elk, moose, badgers and eagles all lived in the countryside around them. My imagination ran wild with thoughts of hunting, trapping, hiking and potential encounters with nature. I could picture myself walking in the wilderness, exploring the forests, carrying binoculars, a rifle strapped to my shoulder.

Soon enough our shopping companions made their way back out to the parking lot and we were on our way. Before getting on the freeway though, Bonnie told me we needed to pick up another pilgrim. He turned out to be a boy about my age, named Joe. He was a Native American who lived in a difficult home, with a drug-addict mother. Bonnie and Jim had fostered him in the past, and she wanted to take him with us on this camping trip. We pulled up at his apartment building, and Bonnie went to the door to fetch him. Soon she came back to the car with a large adolescent in tow, much as she had described him. He was very quiet and said little after our initial introductions.

So together we traveled to the north, toward the Montana line, then turned west toward Mud Lake, before veering north again through the sage brush plateaus, past Lone Pine, skirting the Rocky Mountains which border Idaho and Montana. I had never been that far north before, and the scenery was breathtaking. We were at higher elevations than Idaho Falls, and on either side of the highway we were flanked by lonely mountain ranges and armies of timber. I sat in the back seat with Bonnie, feeling anxious and excited about my future.

When we finally arrived at the Lockes' ranch, after parting paths with our other passengers at the Leadore General Store, it was getting dark. The house was quiet as we walked up onto the porch and entered the front door. I was greeted by a yellow cat and a small black dog, both of whom seemed to have been awaiting my arrival. I set my bag down on the kitchen floor and looked around. The house was beautiful and simple, built out of timber collected and put together by Jim's own hands. I was surrounded by rustically stained wood and furniture and decorations that seemed custom-made for a rancher's home.

We had not been through the door long when a tall figure emerged from one of the back rooms. He was a large and lanky shirtless man, with a bald head, wearing blue jeans. He looked at me and Joe, and then he spoke to his wife.

"You don't listen to a damn thing I say, do you?"

Bonnie ignored his gruff greeting and gave him a hug, rubbing his back with her right hand as she turned and introduced me to her husband Jim. As it turns out, there was something of a storyline leading up to my arrival.

Earlier that week, Jim and Bonnie Lockes had been contacted by the child welfare services about the possibility of offering me a foster home. They had fostered children in the past with good results, and it was thought that the Lockes might have some luck with me. Bonnie was open to the idea, but not Jim. He wanted a break from the responsibilities and headaches involved in foster care. Jim told Bonnie to call them back and decline the opportunity, which she did.

That night, Bonnie had a dream in which God appeared to her

and instructed her that she was to go to Idaho Falls and take me home with her, in spite of Jim's instructions. Startled by the specificity of the dream, Bonnie got up the next day and asked a friend, the manager of the Leadore General Store, to give her a ride. Without saying anything to Jim, she had snuck off to get me, and had decided to bring Joe home as well, so he could attend this camping trip she was hired to cook at.

So I settled in with the Lockes family. The camping trip was not scheduled for a week yet, so Joe and I spent our time hanging around on the ranch. Their place was located in a gorgeous setting, enclosed by the austere mountains of the Continental Divide in the back yard, and the waters of the Lemhi River running past their front door. During the day we helped Jim change sprinkler pipes in the upper fields, walked down to the Lemhi River and fished for trout, rode around on the small motorcycles that were used for getting around, and put out feed for the sheep from the back of Jim's pickup truck.

Leadore is a small community of around 100 souls, spread out over the valley. The sights and sounds of Idaho Falls were replaced by the simple rhythms of country living. A pickup slowly making its way down the gravel road; wooden gates to barbwire fences being opened and shut; the smell and sounds of sheep and livestock; watching cars travel down the distant highway from the front porch; the faint barking of farm dogs; homemade bread and jam; roasting marshmallows by the river at night while the crickets sing; sprinkler pipes moving and locking into place; screen doors attached to rustic homes being opened in the heat of the day.

Time seemed to slow down on the ranch, and the world somehow began to appear less intimidating to me. Waking up early in the morning, and staring across the valley at a nearby mountain range from the quietness of the front porch, sets a tone for the day that cannot be captured in the midst of urban activity. I began to feel like there was very little in this world that I really needed, so long as I could remain in this quiet place.

Jim and Bonnie enjoyed an unstructured kind of religion that was foreign to my experience within the Mormon community. They were openly suspicious of Christian pastors, viewing them as somehow duplicitous in the devil's plan to keep people ensnared in forms and religious rituals. Freedom from structure and the constant expectation of miracles were the twin themes that characterized the Lord's religion on the Lockes' ranch. They rarely saw the need to go to church, as every day was a veritable tent revival meeting for them. Daily experiences provided a seemingly endless supply of occasions to demonstrate the power of God through prayer. They led sinners scattered throughout the Lemhi Valley to a conviction of their sins and the need for salvation through the name of Jesus Christ. Poor people from the area could always come to their ranch to receive prayer, food and as much money as Bonnie could afford to give away at the time.

Bonnie was especially zealous as an evangelist. From time to time she would procure several boxes of Bibles, hook up a trailer to her pickup truck, and travel alone to various places, distributing Bibles and Christian literature on the streets of cities as far away as Portland and Seattle. Jim's main focus was on prayer and healing miracles. He loved to have people stretch out their arms, to demonstrate the unevenness of the length. After a simple prayer, he would then have them repeat the exercise, which never failed to reveal an improvement. His prayers took simple forms.

"Okay. Lord, you see that Paul here has a need for healing. In the name of Jesus we just ask you to restore his body to full health. We claim the healing which you died on the cross to provide for us. We believe that by your stripes we are healed. And we just command the devil to get his filthy hands off of this boy's body. We just know that you are going to work a miracle here. In the powerful name of Jesus. Amen."

Jim's relatively understated spirituality stood in contrast to Bonnie's outrageous enthusiasm. She was given to shouting at the devil when praying.

"Satan, you have no authority in this situation! You know who I am. I've whooped your butt many times before! And in Jesus' name I'm telling you to get out and leave this boy alone! He doesn't belong to you. He's a child of the King! Hallelujah! We praise you Jesus!"

She would then inevitably break into a period of ecstatic glossalalia, or praying in tongues. "Halabashandalahalabandaba!!!" She would go on for several minutes, praying "in the Spirit" for me or whomever she happened to be helping at the time.

I still remember the first time I heard Bonnie pray in tongues. It was during that first week at the ranch. I was staying in Tina's bedroom down in the basement. Joe was sleeping in the spare bedroom next door. Tina was still away at a cheerleading camp and had yet to come home to claim her room. It was dark, and Bonnie had come down to the basement to smoke cigarettes and pray in the darkness, as she often did in the evenings, sometimes well into the late hours of the night. She would sit in her rocking chair with a large Bible in her lap, and smoke, pray and smoke some more. I grew attached to her visits to the basement in the darkness of the night. There was something motherly and comforting about her presence as she sat there in her rocking chair outside my door, something that made me feel safe and loved.

That night she came into the room, sat down on my bed and talked with me, stroking my hair and speaking in soft tones. I don't remember what she talked about. I just listened to the sound of her voice. I was not alone. There was someone to call on, to protect me from the dark presence that had followed me from the nights of my childhood. Someone who felt and smelled feminine. I had not felt the soft touch of a woman's hand for years.

Something within me broke open, and I began to cry. I cried because she reminded me of the care I took for granted as a child. I had no power over my environment. Whether I received nurture or torture was in the hands of the state and its decisions about my care. But now providence, perhaps God, had finally caused me to cross paths with someone who would help and not hurt. And my tears moved her to pray. She prayed for the comfort of God, and she prayed with words beyond the ken of mortal man. I fell asleep as she sat on the bed, listening without understanding, knowing I did not need to understand. In point of fact, I was learning to pray.

Lee Mayer (1986-1988)

At the end of that first week we were scheduled to meet a group in Salmon, who would take us to our camping site in the middle of the White Cloud wilderness area near Stanley, Idaho. This was something like to a Boy Scout gathering, only the group was sponsored by the local Assemblies of God congregation in Salmon. So Bonnie loaded me and Joe into her car, along with another local boy named Johnny Lomax, who was coming along for the camping adventure. Together we traveled up the Lemhi Valley to Salmon, a town of about 3,000 people.

As we pulled into the parking lot of the church, the leader of the group was loading camping equipment into the back of a truck. His name was Lee Mayer. He was a middle aged man, with a black mustache and balding head. Bonnie had already told me a few things about him, including the fact that he had been a college wrestler and high school coach. Bonnie introduced me to him immediately, and there was something about the introduction which struck me as funny, though I could not quite put my finger on it. As we shook hands and chatted, he seemed to be studying me, analyzing me. I shrugged off his curious gaze and put it out of my mind. I had no idea that Bonnie had been speaking with him about taking me as a foster child.

Thus began a camping trip which lasted about a week. I remember little from the experience apart from a few snippets. I remember building things out of wood to practice survival skills and win competitions between the various groups. I remember being tired a lot of the time, and bored with the constant onslaught of events and games. I remember waking up in the middle of the night, remembering I was in a tent, out in the woods. I remember wondering about the presence of black bears around us, and how that thought stirred my spirit. Perhaps my most vivid memory was occasioned by an evangelistic meeting that was held one night around a large campfire.

A speaker had been enlisted to share his testimony of faith with the gathered campers. I don't remember what he spoke of, but I do remember he had known John Wayne personally, and had painted a very skillful portrait of "the Duke" before he died. Tonight, this man's gospel message had a musical accompaniment. Bonnie walked to the center of the encircled campers and admitted that she didn't know how to sing, but that God had told her to sing a song that night. So with a battery powered tape recorder turned on full blast, she put in a tape of some gospel music, and began to sing her heart out. Her willingness to follow God's leading, even at the cost of her own dignity, made such an impression on us that Johnny Lomax and I arose and joined her in the center of the circle while she sang.

Later on, the preacher took the center stage, and made an appeal for those of us who felt the Lord speaking, who wanted to accept Jesus and have our sins forgiven, to come forward and receive prayer. Bonnie was sitting beside me and I felt a prompting to make my life right with God and find salvation. I asked her if she would accompany me if I went forward to accept the Lord into my life. She squeezed my hand

and got up with me. There, along with many other repentant children of various ages and sizes, I confessed my sins, acknowledged my need of forgiveness and invited Jesus to come and be my Lord and Savior. We were all assured that if we had really prayed that prayer sincerely from our hearts, that we were now Christians and could rest secure in the knowledge that we would go to heaven to be with God if we died.

The man then went around and prayed for individual needs. When he came to me, I explained my situation. I told him about my experiences in foster care. Then I told him that what I would like to ask the Lord for, now that I was saved, was a family. I wanted a family who would love me and let me live with them. I said these things with Bonnie standing there, hoping she would sense the call to be that mother I was longing for. The evangelist then said something I will never forget. After listening to my story, he offered no platitudes or promises of blessing.

He put his large, weathered hands on my shoulders and said, "Son, I know it's hard. But probably, you aren't going to get a family. Sometimes the world just doesn't turn out for us the way we wish it would. You're most likely going to have to grow up, become a man, and make a family of your own."

At the end of that week we returned from our camping trip. Not long after, a number of transitions took place. Joe returned to his hopeless life in Idaho Falls. Arrangements had been made with Ruth Hudson for me to pick up the rest of my belongings, along with Mac, and bring them back to the Lockes' ranch. That decision marks one of the deepest regrets of my life.

I should never have returned for Mac. Ruth, despite our tensions, was kind to animals, and there was plenty of room for him in her home. He could have happily lived out the rest of his days with her and her Shih Tzu in Idaho Falls. But the bond I had with that little dog compelled me to take him with me. My love for him blinded me, and deluded me into thinking I would be able to care for him. Time would show that I was in no position to offer Mac a stable home and the care he needed, for such things were in the hands of adults.

Around this time, Tina returned from her cheerleading camp and reclaimed her bedroom, which meant that I had to move over to her brother Troy's old room. Tina was a pretty blond who looked a lot like Bonnie, only 20 years younger. I got along with her well. Like me, she was quiet and reflective. We used to jog together in the evenings, up and down the gravel road that ran past the house, she getting in shape for volleyball and I for the wrestling season. There was never any real romantic chemistry between us, but we soon became friends and enjoyed each other's company.

Eventually Bonnie brought up the subject of me going to live with Lee Mayer in Salmon. We sat on her front porch early one evening, gazing across the valley as the distant mountain range faded from our vision with the setting sun, and weighed the options. She told me I was welcome to stay with her and Jim, but Leadore had a shoddy school system and no wrestling team. I struggled with the choice. I was happy living on their ranch, but I got the sense that she felt I would be better off with the Mayer family. And despite my mediocrity, wrestling was something very much in my teenage blood at the time. After talking for a while, we decided I should move to Salmon.

Salmon is a beautiful little town, flanked by scenic mountains on every side. There is only one main street, which runs through the middle of town, decorated with convenience stores, quaint shops and bars along the way. As you first enter into town from the highway, you get the sense that you are entering a space with many memories. The ghosts of explorers, trappers, Indians and gold miners still haunt the place, stopping to stare at your car as you drive by.

Providence had brought me to Salmon to stay with the Mayer family. Lee Mayer grew up in the southern tip of Idaho near Soda Springs. He was an accomplished wrestler in high school and college, having competed in California on Biola University's team back in the late 60's. Biola University is where he had met his wife Janet. After graduating, they had moved to South America, where they served as Christian missionaries. They both had degrees in education, and had eventually moved back to the states to work as school teachers. Lee had also been employed as a high school wrestling coach for awhile in Salmon, where Janet taught elementary school.

Lee was now unemployed, and had been for some time. He had been fired by the Salmon school district for some reason, and they were currently locked in litigation, suing for unfair dismissal. To try and supplement their family income, Lee worked odd jobs and preached at the local Assemblies of God church from time to time.

The Mayers had three children. A ten-year-old adopted girl named Maya, and two young boys Nate and Benjamin. Nate and Benjamin were extremely successful wrestlers, winning multiple state titles in freestyle competition. Benjamin in particular was a striking little child. Already at age six he had a defined, muscular physique and stunning balance and coordination. Nate did not look as physically impressive, but was very strong and confident for one so young, and actually the more accomplished wrestler. I envied the two boys.

I lived with the Mayers from the beginning of my junior year, nearly to the end of my senior year. It was a dark and sullen time. It is so difficult to recall many clear memories. I get only flashing glimpses of walking to school early in the morning, anxiously registering for classes, staring at the mountains to the west of town.

When I picture life with the Mayers, I feel dull and gloomy and out of place. I can see Lee lying on the floor in front of the TV. The walls are decorated with trophies from his big-game hunts which cost too much money. Mac is vaguely around, but not in my direct line of vision through the window of my foggy memory. The springs in Lee's pickup truck squeak in rhythm with the closing door as I sit staring out the window, the wind blowing in my face. Dreaming of a different kind of world. My experience there culminated in a half-hearted suicide attempt, which led to me being moved to my last foster home. But there were many things that led up to that point. How can I describe my time with Lee Mayer and his family? A number of features from my life stick out as dominant memories.

The first is religion. It is at this point that I became suddenly much more religious than I had ever been in my life. I was baptized and began attending the Assemblies of God church regularly with the Mayer family. I looked forward to church for lots of reasons. I enjoyed discussing the outdoors with the grizzled old hunters in the congregation. I enjoyed the buzz of friendliness with which I was greeted upon entering the church basement in the mornings before the service, with everyone standing around exchanging stories and laughter. I enjoyed the rhythms. Each Sunday we would pull into the gravel parking lot and our feet would crunch on the ground as we made our way toward the entrance of the building. It was especially edifying to crunch across that gravel lot when the air was cold, and the cloudy skies held promise of winter weather.

Their church was a small and friendly congregation, full of loggers, mechanics, ranchers and other working-class people. The pastor graduated from a Pentecostal Bible college and preached practical sermons. I remember in the mornings before church, I would always have at least two cups of coffee, packed with milk and sugar. For some reason my increased religiosity was accompanied by an intense desire for caffeine. This was a religion my mother might have liked. Standing there in the mornings, knowing I could drink as much coffee as I wanted, was tremendously freeing. At the Mayers' house, coffee was rationed, and if more than one pot was consumed in an evening, we had to reuse the coffee grounds.

There weren't many teenagers at that church, but there were a few, including three foster children. They were Native Americans, and had moved in with the Copeland family around the same time I had moved in with the Mayers. I can remember two shy teenage boys, with black hair parted in the middle, feathered on the sides. One was about my age, and one a year older. And I remember having a crush on their slightly younger sister. Like me, they had been tossed from home to home, changing families whenever the circumstances dictated. When I would arrive at church, the boys would often saunter up and chat with me outside the kitchen before Sunday School. We were bound by our vulnerability. It was a casual, but genuine bond, the kind that creates understanding without the need for affection. By the end of that school year, they had moved on to yet another home, in the Idaho Falls area. I hope things turned out okay for them.

The other thing that stands out is a sense of depression. My patterns of isolation did not abate when I moved into the Mayers' house. I continued to feel unwelcome, and spent vast amounts of time in my room. My life seemed destined to repeat familiar patterns at home. Like the Browns, they had a dog, a Samoyed, chained up in the backyard, neglected and uncared for, which bothered me, but I was helpless to do much about it. That following summer between my junior and senior years I was away for a few days at a wrestling camp, and upon returning home was told that the dog had been found in the back yard, dead from who knows what.

"She lived to a good old age," Janet said, somehow seeking to make the neglected end of that poor dog's life more dignified.

Mac was allowed to stay indoors sometimes, but I knew when I was not there he was left outside, or in the garage where they really preferred he stay. I could not afford to give him proper veterinary care. Immunizations and checkups had long since become things of the past. When a heavy log from the firewood pile was dropped on his back one afternoon while unloading a haul, leaving him unable to stand for several days, I was told all we could do was watch and see if he recovered. This was now reality. Despite our limited finances, my mother had always made sure Mac got his shots and was properly cared for.

I did not get along with Maya, their oldest child, at all. She struck me as a precocious, spoiled little girl, who seemed to delight in mocking me whenever the occasion presented itself, and was always searching for opportunities to order me around or get me in trouble. Perhaps under different circumstances we might have gotten along, but her adolescent attitude wore thin on my fractured nerves. I stayed in my room in part just to avoid being around her. She loved to repeat my words back to me, rolling her eyes and displaying her full repertoire of disgusted expressions. So I avoided talking in her presence as much as possible.

The two little boys were easy enough to get along with, but their marked success in wrestling contrasted with my mediocrity, and made me feel inadequate. Lee one time accused me of being jealous of his sons' success on the mat, and he was right. My envy made me sulk, and his pointing out the cause made me sulk all the more.

At school I remained a loner. Though I loosely sat with the wrestlers at lunchtime, I did not socialize with anyone outside of classes and practices. During the off-season, I could often be found alone after school, walking across town towards home, lacking a car or any means of transportation. I can still remember how I would feel as I walked along, conspicuous by my isolation. An adolescent wolf without a pack. At one point the journey was particularly humiliating, as I had to cross the bridge that spanned the Salmon River running through town. The walkway on the side of the bridge was very narrow, which meant that you were close to the cars buzzing by your side. On most of the streets in town I could hide from the traffic by keeping my distance from the road. Cars full of teenagers would buzz by, their faces full of the recognition, sometimes mixed with sympathy, of my place on the social scale. Sometimes kids would honk and jeer as they went past me.

"Get a car, loser."

Kinder students might offer a sympathetic wave. Day after day I walked up the dingy streets of Salmon toward a house that offered no comfort, to be greeted by a faithful dog I could not care for.

I continued to wrestle in my junior and senior years, with mixed success. My junior year was the worst by far. I was losing a lot of weight to make the Varsity squad at the 112-pound weight class, and it was a wasted effort. In practice, when I was not under pressure, I was always competitive with the 119-pound star athlete of our team, Clint May, who went on to become the Idaho state champion in 1988. But my psyche rarely held up when called upon to perform in live competition, and I only won about six matches that whole season. During my senior year I fared a bit better, but it was still all I could do to win just over half my matches at the 125-pound weight, and one tournament in Corvallis, Montana.

I was quite obsessed with wrestling, but I was just too insecure. I had plenty of motivation, and practiced year round, even during the summer months. But motivation has to be combined with natural physical gifts (mine were average), and most importantly, a healthy dose of self-belief. Without the right frame of mind, it is difficult to become an exceptional wrestler. And confidence was not something that my environment provided me with in any great measure.

Poverty was also a factor. The Mayers' dreary house was bleak and tired, with old furniture. Their tattered vehicles were always breaking down. Despite Janet having a teaching job, they had a lot of debts, and were always out of money. When food was running short, we would go to the trashcans behind the local supermarkets and dig out the bread that had been tossed. Janet said all you had to do was pull off the moldy parts, and the bread was just fine to eat. To supplement their food supplies, they picked wild blackberries from the forest for homemade jam. Despite their lack of money though, they always seemed to have the funds to travel around the state for the boys' wrestling tournaments.

And they always seemed to have enough money for Lee to entertain himself with his main obsession in life. The god to whom he paid his most faithful homage. Which was hunting.

In some ways, given my love of the outdoors, living with Lee Mayer would seem like the perfect situation for me. Indeed, he was an avid hunter. He stalked mule deer, antelope, elk and black bears. He spent far more time in the woods than in the search for gainful employment. That first year I stayed with the Mayer family, I accompanied him on countless hunting trips.

I have an abiding image of walking behind Lee Mayer on some trail or logging road, just as the sun is rising. Periodically we stop, as Lee listens for the sounds of creatures moving in the woods. He looks back at me, and puts his finger to his lips to signal silence. I wipe my dripping nose, and we continue.

We saw many mule deer on those trips, including some bucks, though I did not fire a shot until the end of the deer season. You see, Lee always needed to be completely sure he did not want to claim the deer for himself, and by then, it was too late for me to get off a shot. The last day of the season though, I was staked out at a location by myself, and a large mule deer buck came walking by just below my position, about 100 yards off. He was beautiful, walking along the hillside painted with sagebrush and snow, following behind a doe he intended to seduce. I fired once, missing him wildly in my nervous condition, and then the cheap rifle which Lee had supplied me with jammed. Distracted by a doe in the heat of the rut, the buck never even noticed me. So I just sat there with my jammed rifle, and watched that trophy buck calmly walk over the hill and out of my life.

You know, it's a harsh existence that God has allotted to the deer. Their lives destined to end in disease, or starvation, perhaps struggling under the teeth of wild predators, or the bumper of a speeding car, unless they happen to hear the sound of a rifle shot on a hillside. Yet I have never seen a deer that did not appear to be at peace with itself.

One morning Lee and I got up early and headed to the local Smokehouse café for a bite to eat, before heading out in the darkness to our hunting destination. Lee ordered two drinks with his meal.

"I'll take a coffee, and…a hot chocolate too," Lee said as he handed back the menu to the elderly waitress.

Liking the idea, I then ordered the same, only to be disheartened by his disgusted glance in my direction. Somehow, the fact that now I too wanted both coffee, and hot chocolate, had irritated him. His field of vision was so narrow, his nature so petty, that having two drinks with breakfast was a privilege he guarded with jealousy. When we would stop at a convenience store on our hunting trips, he would purchase a soft drink and a snack, and it visibly bothered him when I would ask if I could get something too.

In the fall and the spring, Lee spent a lot of time black bear hunting. He used up gallons and gallons of gas driving around in the mountains, putting out baits to attract unsuspecting bears. The idea was to get the bear coming in to the area where the bait was laid out, so that the hounds (which belonged to a man Lee hunted with) could pick up the scent and tree the animal. I imagined taking a trophy bear on a hunt, and memorializing the rite of passage with a bear rug. I suppose I thought that killing a bear would make me a genuine big-game hunter.

After countless trips with Lee to the baiting sites, we unexpectedly came across a bear in the snow one day late in the fall while out replenishing the bait. Silently, he signaled for me to be still as he looked through his scope. It was frigidly cold, and snow flurries were blowing around us as we crouched in the sagebrush on the edge of the forest. There were actually two bears at the site, unaware of our presence because of the wind direction. One bear was bent over the barrel of rotten bait, while the other stood watch, as though sensing that all was not right with the situation.

Though Lee had been promising me a chance to take a trophy bear all season, he quickly fired off three rapid shots. The closest bruin, uneasily standing guard, collapsed under the hail of bullets and did not move from the spot, while the other made a hasty exit. Upon approaching the downed beast, already expired, it quickly became apparent that it was just an average sized adult. He sheepishly apologized to me, and told me he had gotten carried away in his excitement.

"That should have been your bear," he said with a grimace.

I looked sadly at the slain animal, and shrugged my shoulders. As a young man's first bear, its death might have meant something. But as it was, it just seemed like killing. Lee Mayer had murdered a bear in cold blood.

Bears were not the only victims. I was somehow supposed to believe that porcupines are the mortal enemies of all true hunters. Lee, and the men he hunted with, always killed them whenever they came across them, shooting them and leaving their dying carcasses by the side of the road. For some reason those plodding, hapless animals always showed up to greet us as we drove along isolated logging roads.

Once I naively asked, "Why do you always have to shoot the porcupines?"

Lee stared ahead with a firm grimace as he drove.

"Because the dogs run into them and get their mouths full of quills," he assured himself. "Besides, don't you know they kill all the trees?"

Yet, as I watched this spectacle unfold, I knew better. Here were men, grown men with wives and families and pets at home, who just enjoyed pouring bullets into slow, helpless creatures. What must the world seem like to a porcupine, when he crosses paths with men, men with guns and bullets, but bereft of heart and soul?

After one particularly ugly incident, in which a porcupine was knocked senseless with rocks until a gun could be loaded to finish it off, I said to Lee as he climbed back into the pickup, "You guys are animals." Their thirst for blood spoiled my idyllic vision of hunting and the outdoors, so profoundly that I have never really recovered. Whatever this was, it was not a respectful participation in nature's patterns and cycles.

Toward the end of my senior year, I was drowning in a sea of hopelessness. All around me was darkness. The futility of life was draining away my will to go on. Though the Mayers were not abusive, they offered no sense of love or nurture. It was perhaps the emotional low point of my teenage experience.

One afternoon I was alone at the house, and I guess I decided I had had enough. I didn't want to be like this anymore, and there was only one path of escape. I knew I did not have the determination to put a loaded gun to my head and pull the trigger. I had already tried to conjure up the courage to do that once before. So I walked down the hallway past my room, and found my way to the bathroom medicine cabinet.

I looked down to my left at the dingy carpet, then in front of me at the cheap mirror above the sink. An uncaring and lethargic-looking boy was staring at me. He offered no comfort. He refused to tell me what to do, but only watched as I poured out a bunch of painkillers into my hand, and numbly swallowed them.

I then walked into the living room, picked up the phone from the counter next to the kitchen area, and called Bonnie. "I need to talk to you. It's important."

I had chosen a day when I knew she was in town visiting her mother. I suppose I wanted her to see how deeply I had suffered from living with the Mayers. I wanted her to come and save me. Bonnie came over to the house about thirty minutes later.

I got into her car and announced, "I swallowed a bunch of pills."

"Son of a bitch," she cursed, and hit the gas petal. "How many did you take?"

All I could say was a handful.

Bonnie made a decision as she drove. Rather than take me to the hospital, which maybe she should have done, she immediately began to pray over me, asking for the Lord to heal my body. I remember sitting in the car listening to her pray, but the rest of the day is lost in fog. Whatever the reason, I suffered no permanent effects from the stunt, other than a couple of days of grogginess and a very sore stomach.

That week, upon consultation with the child welfare authorities, the decision was made for me to move in with another family I had come to know through a local church youth group. Their name was Bud and Jan Summers. My last attempt to find my way back to the Lockes' ranch, with its idyllic scenery and slow, country rhythms, had failed.

Senior Year (1987-1988)

In the summer prior to my senior year, Bonnie had invited me to attend a family camp in Montana that was organized by the local Foursquare Gospel church in town. The name of the congregation was Faith Bible Chapel, and its pastor was a plump, bearded man by the name of Greg Middlebrook. Greg was a graduate of the Foursquare Church's denominational school, Life Pacific College, and had gone on to earn his master's degree in divinity at Ashland Theological Seminary in Ohio. He was a friendly, soft-spoken man with striking musical gifts. During my time at that camp, I also became acquainted with the volunteer youth pastors of Faith Bible Chapel, Bud and Jan Summers. They invited me to visit their church, and soon I was spending more time with them on Sundays than with the Mayers.

The meetings at Faith Bible Chapel were more lively than anything I had previously experienced, with upbeat music that put a spring in your step and made you want to clap your hands. Everywhere around you during the worship services people would be clapping and hopping and raising their hands in enthusiastic praise to God. Sometimes folks would break out into words of prophecy, or stretches of ecstatic tongue speaking. Time was always allotted during the service to pray for the sick, seeking after the healing power of God.

Though I was not given much to outward demonstration, even as a teenager, the catchy tunes and praise choruses made my heart beat faster. Before the church meeting, Rev. Middlebrook would get together with a group of people in his office to pray for the Holy Spirit's leading. After I had attended there for a while, he started inviting me to join those special gatherings. I felt very privileged, like I was being singled out as having some special promise or call of God on my life.

I attended the youth group meetings that were held on Sunday afternoons before the evening service. There, Bud and Jan Summers diligently led a small group of teenagers in discussions of topics ranging from prayer, to Bible study to the temptations of sex and drugs. Knowing what I did of the makeup of our little group, it was evident to me that my fellow attendees were much more familiar with sex and drugs than the mysteries of prayer and Bible study. I felt like I was the only one who took the rules of holy Christian living seriously outside the walls of the church. I tried to pray every day, and began to read the Bible frequently. Given my social patterns, staying away from the temptations of parties and their attendant sins was easy for me.

Soon I started checking out books from the church library, learning all that I could about scripture, Christian doctrine, and tips for "refuting" false religions and leading people to Christ. Rev. Middlebrook noticed these patterns in my studies, and began to take me under his wing, encouraging me in my personal "walk with the Lord."

When my emotional state deteriorated to such an extent that I made that half-hearted suicide attempt late in my senior year, Bud and Jan opened up their home to me. I got along well with their son Jeff, who was the same age as I. He was a tall, handsome basketball player, with a calm demeanor and affable temperament. My first couple of days at their house were spent recovering from the grogginess and sore stomach caused by my pill overdose, but soon afterwards I began to settle in to the normal rhythms of their family.

I would get up early for school with Jeff, and Jan would typically have some sort of breakfast prepared by the time we had showered. Pancakes with chocolate chips were a household favorite. I quickly noticed that Jeff brushed his teeth every morning, and suddenly realized that I had almost never brushed my teeth in 17 years. Following his lead, I began to brush with him.

Jeff was never a brother to me, but he did give me a glimpse of what having a brother might have been like. He shared his parents' time and attention with me at meals. He encouraged me to get out of bed when the alarm clock in our room went off in the morning. He let me drive around with him, up and down the country roads, in the family pickup truck. We especially enjoyed going to the county dump with the trash, talking in the truck along the way. He let me hang around with him and his girlfriend Julie, when they would no doubt have preferred to be alone. He shared his experiences with sex and drugs, assuring me I should be thankful I had not walked his path (by the end of his senior year he too had become a born-again Christian). We discussed our plans for the future. Jeff was firmly committed to going into the military after graduation, where he planned to save enough money for college.

Bud and Jan were a hard-working couple. They struck an odd pose. Bud was a short, stocky man with bulging muscles, while Jan was tall, broad-shouldered, large-boned, thin and lanky in her younger years. They had tried their hand at farming down in Mud Lake before financial hardships forced them to give it up. Now they lived a challenging life somewhere near the very bottom of the middle class. Bud worked with his hands as a day laborer on a farm. Jan as an office secretary for a local business. Between their two full-time jobs, they barely managed to scrape together enough money each month to stay up on their mortgage and car payments.

The Summers were my final foster family, and my relationship with them has always been ambivalent and hard to define. On the one hand, more than any other foster family, they verbally encouraged me to think of myself as one of their kids. They openly referred to me as their new "son" when introducing me to other people, and made other subtle gestures to make me feel included as best they could. But I found that, by this time, I had lost my capacity to be a son to anyone.

Though I tried, I could never bring myself to think of Jan as my "mom," or Bud as my "dad." Yes, initially, I played along, and would purchase cards for them on Mothers' Day and Fathers' Day. But I gave up the practice after a year or two without a word being exchanged between us. We all knew it was a charade. I got along with them well enough, but our relationship has never been overly close.

I remember very little from that year, though the senior prom stands out in my mind. Not because I attended it of course. Rather I helped some mischievous friends (older bachelor-types named Doug and Dave, who knew Bud and Jan from church connections) to fill up Jeff's flashy yellow sports car (which he had borrowed from Dave for the prom) with balloons, while he was inside the school dancing with his girlfriend Julie.

I remember on that same night, the three of us laid our hands on the walls of one of the local bars in town, and prayed that God would win a victory over Satan by putting the bar out of business. Mostly though, we just rode around town together that night, laughing at our own silly humor, and trying to convince ourselves we did not long for the company of beautiful women.

Apart from my kissing sessions with young Gayelynn, and my fleeting North Carolina romance with Beth, I had no teenage experiences with girls to reminisce upon. I had a few crushes, of course. A tall, thin, pot-smoking, heavy metal fanatic blond comes to mind, whose locker was next to me; and an athletic blond who was famous in the school for her success in rodeo competitions. I never uttered more than half a sentence to either girl. I had no pool of confidence, no stockpile of brash attitude, and no financial resources that might have given me the initiative to pursue teenage romances. Lacking such things, the only other way to earn affection it seemed, was to get into a lot of trouble, and appeal to some hapless girl's desire to change me. Lacking both charisma and a rebellious nature, I was doomed to a life of hormonal isolation.

I did have one almost romantic experience during my time at Salmon High School. Bonnie's daughter Tina called me on the phone out of the blue one afternoon, and suggested we go out for a night on the town. It was the only official "date" I had in high school. I found her invitation strange, as I had never sensed any chemistry between us. Nonetheless, she drove up on a Friday night in her old blue car and came to the door. Lee winked at me as I walked out of the house, though I had protested that this was only a friendly venture.

She was acting so strangely that evening. At one point she commented to me that there was another young man in town she was attracted to, but he was dating some older woman.

"Why would he want to go out with a woman her age?" she asked me.

I shrugged, unsure why we were engaged in this line of communication.

She continued. "Just because she will give him all the sex he wants? Well, so would I, and I'm young and still full of energy."

She looked over at me and said, "That's what I like about you. You're nice, not like these other guys I end up dating. You know what I mean?"

I gulped, uncertain what to do about her lumping me in the same category with the *other guys* she had gone out with.

"Yeah, I don't know," I lamely responded, with a cracked voice, making no attempt to follow up on that line of conversation.

Had I been a different person, had I allowed my hormones to fill me with confidence rather than fear, I might have replied with, "If you like me so much, how come we haven't ever kissed?" Or some similarly foolish and yet bold remark. Instead I stared out the window in front of me, looking at the cars and the lights going past us as we drove for hours up and down Main Street.

Eventually, we made our way to a local bar, where Tina managed to get the bartender to illegally serve us each several glasses of Pink Schnapps. After that, I remember very little. Later she dropped me off, and I remember laying there on my bed, with the ceiling above me spinning in circles. I only got a couple of hours of sleep, as I had to be up with Lee at 4am for a bear hunting trip. Despite my condition, I got up and accompanied him. What Tina's motives were on that night remains a mystery to me. It was an anomaly in our friendship, and never repeated.

At some point during that summer, Doug and Dave accompanied a group from our church to a Christian conference in Kalispell, Montana, sponsored by YWAM (Youth With A Mission). The singer Sheila Walsh was performing there, as was the "Christian rock" group Petra. We stayed in a former military facility, where Japanese citizens had been interred during World War II, now converted to a YWAM base.

During the days, we attended workshops, addressing topics such as Bible study, evangelism, worship and popular eschatology. One speaker laid out what was intended to be a carefully reasoned case as to why Jesus would most likely return before the year 1988 was finished. I remember little of the content of those workshops, though during one of them (the one focused on 1988 I think), I distinctly remember

Doug nearly killing me with laughter as he crunched ice between his teeth, while pressing either side of his head with his hands, to give the impression that he was crushing his own skull. There was something beautiful about this twenty-nine-year-old bachelor's refusal to grow up and accept adulthood.

Throughout the trip Doug was shamelessly hitting on one of the high school girls name Lori, who was attending the event with our youth group. Doug acquiesced when she demanded he show her how many push-ups he could do, and otherwise performed for her like a lovesick teenager. Upon returning to Salmon he called her on the phone with me standing there, nervous, but trying to appear composed. You had to love him, pity him, and feel a little disturbed by his behavior all at the same time.

Life with the Summers was non-dramatic in comparison with my other foster experiences. There were no tensions between me and Jeff. There was no pornography. Bud was nice to me. They seemed happy to have Mac with them for the time being (though that would later change). They lived in a nice house out in the country, where there was plenty of room to walk and think.

I would often walk around in the hills above their house, trying to find myself. I was usually carrying Bud's weathered old .22, not because I was intent on hunting, but because carrying the rifle while I wandered, made me feel like something I wanted to be. Perhaps it kept alive the idyllic vision of the roaming hunter as nature-loving outdoorsman, which Lee Mayer and his porcupine-murdering friends had not been able to entirely extinguish. But, no matter how far I walked, I could not escape that sense of disorientation that has followed me since the death of my mother.

As the end of my senior year approached, I had to decide what to do with myself. My modest improvements as a wrestler that year had opened up a window of opportunity for me to attend Pacific Lutheran

University in the state of Washington, where I was offered a partial wrestling scholarship. My other option was to join the military. The Army recruiters were calling me every day, trying their best to make me feel valuable, urging me to make a final commitment to my country. The college funds that were offered through military service made it tempting. But something was holding me back. Meanwhile at church, Rev. Middlebrook was encouraging me to consider God's call upon my life, and was pointing me in the direction of Life Pacific College in Los Angeles (named LIFE Bible College in those days).

Then one afternoon I received a call from Jim Hazewinkel, who introduced himself as the head wrestling coach at a small college in Owatonna, Minnesota—Pillsbury Baptist Bible College, one of the Christian colleges to which I had sent out inquiries. I learned that Coach Hazewinkel (and his twin brother) had the distinction of having wrestled for two Olympic teams. Though he could offer me no formal scholarship due to the college's limited budget, he assured me he could get me lined up with on-campus employment to help with my financial needs. By the time I hung up the phone, I knew I would be moving to Minnesota in the fall.

Sojourning Among the Baptists (1988-1989)

When August of 1988 arrived, I found myself in a car with Jan, riding up to Missoula, Montana to catch a flight to Minneapolis. I can remember her hugging me in the airport terminal, telling me how proud everyone was of my accomplishment. But I felt almost embarrassed to be headed to college. Even today, as a college professor, I often feel like I have somehow tricked fate, and failed to live down to my appointed destiny.

Boys who grow up the way I did do not go to college, much less advance to graduate and doctoral level education. Don't I know that?

I blush when people address me as "Dr. Owen," as though, little known to them, I have stolen the identity of some good man and am now living a life under false pretenses, masquerading as a scholar.

Truth be told, I felt like it was Jeff who should be getting ready for his first semester, perhaps at Idaho State University or some similar institution. Jeff was a more rounded student, socially adept, gifted at basketball, got better grades. While I was "bookish" and an avid reader, my grades, like my athletic skills, always meandered in the realm of mediocrity, with occasional hints of promise. Nonetheless, providence seems to delight in confounding the best laid plans and expectations of men, and thus it was I who was now boarding a plane to Minnesota, headed off to college. Jeff, a month or so earlier, had boarded a flight to Georgia, where he was undergoing his basic training in the Army.

I was picked up at the airport in Minneapolis by two handsome students from Pillsbury, dressed in sharp clothes and dress jackets. I immediately felt sheepish about my own appearance, having shown up in sneakers, old faded jeans and a t-shirt. The more talkative of the two was named Chad, who seemed to be the leader. I learned he was the student body president. He was charming, with short blond hair and a muscular build. Both young men greeted me with a firm handshake, and soon we were on our way. As we left the airport and made our way to Owatonna, they asked me questions about my upbringing and what had led me to pick Pillsbury. I explained to them that I wanted to attend a Christian college, and had been attracted to their school because of Coach Hazewinkel.

In the course of the conversation, the subject of my church involvement came up. As I explained the features of my home church, Faith Bible Chapel, the quieter of the two (an aristocratic-looking boy with short, dark hair, a prominent chin, and glasses) shot a nervous glance in Chad's direction from the front seat.

"You realize of course, that Pillsbury is a *Baptist* college. I think you'll find it quite different from the sort of church experience you seem familiar with," Chad helpfully offered. I knew that Baptists were different from Pentecostals, but I had no idea just how radical the shift would prove to be. I would soon find myself thrust into a distinctive subculture, in which time seemed to stand still, or rather regress, to the 1950's perhaps.

Pillsbury's identity was wrapped up in the distinctive convictions of Christian fundamentalism. They shunned all forms of interdenominational cooperation, modernist viewpoints, popular Bible translations (other than the King James Version), and worldly associations. Through requisite church attendance at an approved Independent Baptist congregation, strict dress codes (no jeans allowed in classes or chapel, and only modest dresses for girls) and firmly enforced standards of conduct (forbidding all forms of dancing, gambling, movie attendance, smoking and similar sins), the college certainly was successful in creating a distinctive ethos.

I was delivered safely to the campus early enough in the afternoon (it was a Sunday) to make it to the evening service at one of the more popular Baptist churches in town. The church had a school bus that arrived at the campus and picked up all the students who needed transportation. When 5:30pm rolled around, I stepped into a new world. Nervous, self-conscious and unsure of my expectations, I tried my best to hide from my fears by immersing myself within the crowds of students. Standing quietly in line with a group, awaiting our ride to church, I could hope to escape the notice of my college peers, much like a Zebra hiding in numbers within the herd while crossing a crocodile-infested river.

Upon arrival, I followed the lines into the large brick building, and tried to pretend I fit in with the surroundings, as though I were familiar with their strange hymns, which they sang with a distinctive tone and pace that threw me just slightly off guard. Everything, from the announcements to the preaching, to the singing, to the tone of the prayers, was designed to create within us a sense of distinctive Baptist identity. It was an alternate universe, quietly operating, like a monastery, in the midst of the world's sin and confusion. The patterns of dress, the stock expressions, the subtleties of gaze and laughter, all created within me an immediate sense that I had stumbled into a world I had not been prepared for. I was far from the joviality, earthiness and working-class atmosphere that had characterized my worship experiences among the

Pentecostals. The freedom of the Spirit was replaced here with the calmness of conformity.

On the bus ride home, I sat next to another handsome lad with an aristocratic chin (I seemed to be surrounded by them) and serious demeanor. All too soon, once we had exchanged formalities, he sensed I was not one of them, and asked about my scruples concerning movie attendance. I told him I thought everyone pretty much had to make up their own mind whether or not a particular movie was suitable for viewing.

"If it offends your conscience, you shouldn't watch it," I offered.

"So then, you *are* willing to watch movies with at least some filth, huh?" he asked rhetorically. "Not me," he continued. "Job said, 'I have made a covenant with mine eyes. How then can I gaze at a virgin?' That settles it for me."

He seemed very confident of his position. I considered his argument, still unsure whether Job's commitment not to "gaze at a virgin" proved much of anything about watching R-rated movies. But, it seemed like a plausible enough deduction from the cited text, so I grew quiet.

The Pillsbury campus was modest in size, but quite beautiful. Large, spacious oak trees, carefully landscaped lawns (not to be walked on), and grand brick buildings surrounded me on all sides. I was also struck by the plethora of beautiful young women, who walked in herds among their own kind, sometimes offering the reward of a smile and a giggle while walking by. They were always decorated with colorful dresses, and often walked arm in arm while traveling across campus, as though needing to protect one another from frivolous talk and worldly temptations.

Increasingly I found a longing for female companionship building up from somewhere deep within. Sitting quietly next to a girl on the bus trip to church could inspire enough plans to occupy my imagination for days, even if we barely exchanged a word. My courses that first year consisted mostly of General Education requirements, and I developed a horrible, childish crush on my English professor, a graceful Japanese-American lady who was enticingly single. I developed an abundance of strategies to create reasons for talking to her after class, and occasionally in the foyer at the church we both attended.

The social gathering spot at Pillsbury was a charming little site in the basement of Old Main (one of the key buildings on campus, where a lot of administrative offices were located). It was apparently intended to reflect the Rockwellian atmosphere of a quaint American drugstore in the 1950's, with ice cream, hot drinks and a variety of tasty snacks. Though I had very little money, I sometimes managed to scrape together enough to buy an ice cream. From time to time I would be rewarded with chats with the pretty girls who seemed to haunt the place. They always struck me as elusive creatures, mirages in the desert. I got the sense that they would be there, only as long as I did not reach out for them, in which case they would suddenly vanish like a vapor. Lacking both self-esteem and money for dates, I passed through the course of that year without making any overt attempts to formalize a romance.

My memories from Pillsbury are full of the winter and the bitter cold. Minnesota winters are windy and harsh, with lots and lots of snow. Many journeys through the cold, from classroom to classroom, from dorm to eating hall, from eating hall to wrestling mat, are burned into my psyche. Every step of progress came at a cost, every journey cost you something, when you traveled outside in 20-degrees-below-zero conditions, strong winds blowing at you with fury, as though to weaken your resolve to leave your bed in the morning.

During the Christmas break I made arrangements to ride a Greyhound bus to Salmon, Idaho and back. It was a strange and surreal journey, like a dream, with long stretches of quiet winter countryside passing by my gaze, punctuated by stops and bathroom breaks. Kind of like life, really. Slowly but surely, even while sitting on that bus, I was growing stronger, deepening in resolve, riding through the storms and uncertainties of my life into a more settled future. I was being carried forward through time as much as through distance. The path of progress takes some through the lands of privilege and pleasure, but for most of us it involves a simple journey of discovery that requires us to only sit and wait time out, biding the hours while we age and grow, being prepared for success simply by our capacity to continue on.

Upon the return trip, winter storms left us stranded somewhere in North Dakota, and I spent three difficult days moving back and forth from the Greyhound bus (where there was warmth from the always-running engine), and a café, where there was little heat, but plenty of light, food and society. I ate now and then, and slept in the café booths. I spent most of my time watching the behavior of the people around me, listening to their conversations, waiting for the storms to pass.

Eventually we continued on our way, but not before I had seen the mysteries that can only come from the study of the poor (for who else would be stranded in that situation, choosing between the bus and the booth). The quietness of the elderly, the tension of young couples, the tears of small children who have too little to eat, the anxiety of single mothers, the loneliness of crowds, the hopelessness of waitresses who have lost their dreams and themselves, the weariness of people who can't seem to get to their destination and are forgetting where that even was.

My roommate back at Pillsbury was a junior named John. He was a stocky young man with black hair, the son of a Baptist church music minister. John worked the late shift at Pizza Hut, which had its benefits, as he would often bring home leftovers that we hungrily devoured. John had a friendly and thoughtful personality, and I can't recall a single argument with him the whole year we shared that dorm room. I do remember him having very strong body odor, which always struck me as I was lying in bed, when he would be moving about. Sometimes we would commit small acts of rebellion together, such as listening to forbidden forms of Christian music in the seclusion of our room, perhaps some catchy tune with guitars and drums or a faster rhythm than the accepted Baptist hymns. John confessed he had a liking for a nice Baptist girl at church. I in turn confessed my infatuation with the English professor, much to his delight and amusement.

The wrestling coach at Pillsbury, Jim Hazewinkel, was a wonderful man. He was short, middle-aged, with a balding head and stocky frame, about 150 pounds of solid muscle. Full of life, built like a tank, he loved to wrestle college kids of all sizes during practice, laughing with great amusement, like a child being tickled, if any student came close to taking him down or scoring points on him. He clearly loved the sport of wrestling, and was always a model of good Christian character.

I injured my elbow badly, hyper-extending it during practice early on, and I missed out on much of the first half of the season. When I came back after the Christmas break, my elbow was still not 100 percent, but it was healed enough to justify returning to competition. Though I won only slightly over half of my matches as a freshman at Pillsbury, I had a good finish, placing third at the NCCAA (National Christian College Athletic Association) finals in Kankakee, Illinois at the 126-pound weight. Another freshman, named Jim Gruenwald, who competed for Maranatha Bible College in Wisconsin, won the national title at my weight that year. He would go on to become a two-time Olympian, and one of the top-ranked wrestlers in the world. But that would be my last year as a competitive wrestler. I had accomplished all I was ever going to in the sport.

As time went on, it became increasingly clear that I was not a good fit for Pillsbury. Though my grades were good, and I enjoyed my classes, I could never acclimate to my Fundamentalist surroundings. I had many conversations with students that year, and some with faculty and staff, in which well-meaning people attempted to persuade me to leave behind my Pentecostal past, and embrace their Baptist point of view. Though I would eventually grow out of the soil of Pentecostal spirituality, and turn into a different kind of plant entirely, the time was not yet ripe for that transformation, and I never had the makings of a Baptist in any case. Even at that age, I was too open to the spirit of modernity, too ecumenical at heart, too captivated by the breath of new learning and scholarship (which I was only beginning to acquaint myself with as a fledgling student of the Bible and theology), essentially too inclined to live out my faith on the edge of the world and its dangers to find a permanent place among them.

During the Christmas break, while I was visiting Bud and Jan, I had attended a conference in Denver with our church youth group. There, while participating in the break-out sessions and worship services with other teenagers from our church, I decided that God was taking me in a different direction. The theme for the Foursquare youth conference that year was "Choose the Call," and I believed God was placing a call upon my life to pursue an academic ministry.

In consultation with my pastor back home (Rev. Middlebrook), I decided to transfer to Life Pacific College, starting my sophomore year. I would enroll in their Bachelor of Arts program, with a concentration in biblical languages, so I could study Greek and Hebrew, and prepare for whatever God wanted of me as a teacher and a scholar. So, when the fall of 1989 arrived, I was once again riding in a car with Jan, but this time we were headed south, to Los Angeles.

Living in California (1989-1993)

In August of 1989, Jan dropped me off at the campus of Life Pacific College in the Echo Park neighborhood of Los Angeles. It was a bewildering new experience for me on many levels. The freeway traffic was something I had never encountered before, and the hustle and bustle of the city streets created an overload of stimuli for someone of my background. I was plunged into a cement jungle, totally out of my element, intimidated. Jan had some relatives in southern California to meet up with, so not long after she helped me unload my things and settle into my dorm room, she was off.

My roommate was already settled in. He was a tall, large-boned young man, in his mid-20's named Roy Higginbotham. He came from Montana, which is probably why we were put together. He had long, reddish-brown hair and scruffy clothes. Clearly, like me, he had few financial resources at his disposal. Neither of us had a car and we were both eager to secure employment so that we could stay enrolled in school beyond one semester. I found out that prior to coming to the college, he had been a drug dealer in his hometown, before he found

God and got his life straight. After chatting, we decided to stretch our legs and wander down the street to the local McDonald's. As we walked, I observed my surroundings.

The weather was hot, even in the early evening, and the sun beat down mercilessly onto our world of cement and steel. People walked past us on every side. I saw madmen dressed in rags and talking to themselves, Mexican gang-members with bandanas and hard faces, stressed businessmen in suits, homeless people rummaging through trash cans, nameless and shapeless strangers in herds rushing by without a word or glance. Roy had arrived a few days earlier, and explained how only a couple of days ago there had been a shooting, witnessed by several students, outside this very McDonald's we were walking toward. The idea of people shooting each other in broad daylight on a public street was bewildering to me. It sounded more like the Old West than modern civilization. We arrived safely though, and shared more of our personal journeys and our hopes as I munched on a Big Mac, fries and a Coke. I noticed Roy just ordered some fries and a glass of water.

The following week I signed up for my schedule of classes at the old Echo Park campus. My new course of study involved an assortment of lectures dealing with biblical literature, theology and issues in Christian ministry. Though I was signed up for the biblical languages concentration in my degree program, all students at the college majored in Bible and theology, with varying emphases depending on their path of ministry. Students could choose from tracks that focused on pastoral ministry, biblical languages, church education, elementary school education or the mission field. I found the atmosphere refreshing and academically challenging. Lively worship services, full of youthful vitality and energy, were held throughout the week to balance academic life with the development of a personal walk with God. I immediately felt that I had made the right choice, and believed God had prepared this place just for me.

Attending chapel was always powerful. You entered from the back street, which ran parallel to Glendale Boulevard on the front of the campus. My typical memory has me along that street, walking in the sunshine, observant of the sights and sounds of the Hispanic neighborhood around us. The palm trees of Echo Park are directly behind me. On every side, other students are chattering about their classes. I walk alone, lost in my thoughts, or sometimes with an acquaintance, continuing a conversation begun in the preceding class.

Upon entering the chapel, the auditorium is abuzz with enthusiasm, as students find their seats. I sit down, in the area where the professors tended to congregate, and watch, waiting for the signal that chapel is beginning. For some reason, I always find myself in the position of watching, studying, taking in my surroundings. It is as though college, like my world in general, is a fish tank full of startling creatures swimming around me. I derive energy simply by being there, knowing that while I will never mingle with the college crowd, I am playing my own part, equally vital, in the vast scheme of things.

I needed a job, or I would be running out of money very quickly. I heard a rumor that the Pioneer supermarket around the corner was hiring bag boys, so I walked over there and requested an application. I spoke with the manager (a Chinese-American man named Henry) and was hired on the spot. I paid my way through school that year, partly through Pell Grants and other financial aids, and partly through working as many hours as I could at that supermarket. It was not the most exciting work, but neither was it particularly difficult, and I just felt lucky to land a job within walking distance of the campus. My roommate Roy found a job doing some sort of backbreaking work, loading trucks at "the docks." He would show up at the selected site with other eager workers and hope to be picked that night by the foreman.

The most difficult aspect of my experience that year was the feeling of containment. Lacking a car, it was difficult to get anywhere, and I found the sights, smells and sounds of the inner city suffocating. Smog, car exhaust, trash, human waste, the honking of horns, street lights, screeching tires and sulking crowds surrounded me on every side.

Where did all these people come from, and why did they all congregate here?

Any opportunity to get out and away from the campus was gladly accepted, whether it was a trip to the beach with other students, an offer of a ride to visit a local church, or a college ministry event.

Early on I made friends with Mike Murphy, from Bishop, California. We were united by our common interest in Mormonism. Mike had a car, which he used to travel back and forth to his hometown to visit his girlfriend (with whom he had an agonizing obsession) on weekends, and during the week he would sometimes take me out with him to drive around. We drove down to the beach, and explored the streets of Hollywood and downtown LA at night. The lights and activity of the city fascinated both of us. Driving into Hollywood after dark gave us a glimpse of a nightlife that we were committed to abstaining from as born-again Christians, yet it plainly held our interest.

Mike was especially fond of cruising Hollywood for prostitutes, not to pay for their services, but simply for the thrill of spotting them. Transvestite prostitutes dressed in drag seemed to be worth extra bonus points. We engaged in prostitute-spotting at night much like a tourist might take note of wildlife while traveling through Yellowstone National Park.

"There's one. See her, right over there? She's directly behind that pickup, standing with her back against the wall."

"Oh yes! I see her. I see her. Are you sure it's a female?"

As I got to know more of the other students, I found they had interesting stories. Again and again, in the dorms, in the classes, and during chapel services, I heard kids share their testimonies of how they had escaped the clutches of sin and found God. Sometimes through dreams, sometimes through tragedies, often through the prayers of family members and friends. Occasionally, one might find a student who had grown up in a Christian home, never ensnared by Satan's schemes, but they seemed to be the exception. It was those whose lives were littered with bad choices, pain, and struggle who tended to feel called by God to full-time Christian ministry.

One such student was an older enrollee (probably about 30 at the time) named Ray Hedlund. Ray was originally from Chicago, but had been living near Sun Valley, Idaho in the years prior to attending college. He was a landscaper by trade, who had lived a hard life of partying and drug abuse prior to his conversion. Because he too had moved to LA from Idaho, we soon got to know each other.

Ray was a character. He had muscular arms and legs, which were somewhat oddly attached to his torso and expanding belly. His hair was red and thinning, and he had prominent nostrils. He often sniffed deeply from his right nostril just prior to speaking, with his nasal Chicago accent. I got to know Ray, traveling back and forth with him from LA to Idaho for breaks and visits. He was the polar opposite of me, not given to reading or study. A man of action, not words. Good with his hands, adept at building and repairing things. We got along well, perhaps each of us seeing in the other something to be jealous of.

I loved the trips to and from Idaho. The feel of excitement that would build on the day of departure was invigorating. Getting into the car, making our way out of the LA traffic, moving along the freeway, each foot of pavement a little bit closer to freedom, a little further from the cement prison which trapped us most of the year. Soon, we are east of Ontario and Upland and headed toward the serenity of the California desert. As lights and buildings give way to the sagebrush, I feel my heart rate slowing down, my reason returning, slowly remembering that there are still spaces out there, places not filled with cement, steel and smog.

Once we crossed the border into Nevada, we would stop at State Line and go into the casino to fill our stomachs with good food. There we were entertained by the lights and sounds of slot machines, and the sights of crowds moving among the shadows, coming from who knows where, milling about at night for reasons known only to themselves. Then we would again be on our way, traveling east through Las Vegas, and then north through the desert, answering the call to nestle in the arms of our mountain homeland for a time of rest. While in Idaho I felt like a visitor from a strange world. Like Superman, visiting mortals on planet earth, with tales to tell of worlds beyond their ken.

The following year the college campus relocated to San Dimas, a sprawling California suburb about 30 minutes to the east of Los Angeles. The move caused me some degree of angst, as I still had no car, and worried how I would get around the area. I was not likely to find another Pioneer Supermarket to work at within easy walking distance.

On a whim, I visited the local high school, literally across the street, and found out that they were searching for an assistant wrestling coach. I interviewed and was immediately hired. In addition to the money I had saved from working the previous summer, the coaching job paid enough to get me by that first year at the new campus. I continued to coach at San Dimas High School for the next three years until I graduated. The summer of 1991 brought me my first car, an AMC Concord, bought for $600, which made getting around a lot easier. I worked several other jobs to get me by, including the college library, the financial aid office and a local public library in Diamond Bar in the evenings.

I came to know many good people during those years. I grew especially close to Prof. Larry Powers, a thin, bearded man with a dignified bearing, who was my first Greek professor, and a model of courtesy and scholarship. His lectures inspired me to pursue excellence in my studies, and his encouraging words made me believe I had the marks of a successful scholar. Profs. Chuck and Barbara Middlebrook (the parents of my hometown pastor), who lectured in the areas of church history and theology, took me under their wing in an almost parental way, and offered care and pastoral attention, as I made the difficult journey from adolescence into adulthood.

Throughout my years at the college, I continued to attend the same church, Angelus Temple in Echo Park. This was the church founded by the famous evangelist and miracle-healer, Aimee Semple McPherson. The huge, white, domed structure captivated me. I loved to wander its haunted rooms and corridors. I would catch a ride to church from San Dimas in the mornings, and then stay there until the evening service, meandering about in the quiet solitude of the large, empty church building, or resting in one of the nearby dorm rooms now belonging to Angelus Temple's Hispanic Bible Institute. Sometimes I would venture outside, and wander around the haunts of my old neighborhood, taking in the fountains and ice cream stands of Echo Park, families walking in the sunshine with their children, homeless people sleeping on benches, young men playing touch football in the grass, and the ever-present angry youths walking in small groups among the crowds.

I spent those Sunday afternoons in Echo Park reading and reflecting, watching, walking, and wondering about the meaning of my life. I was growing accustomed to quietness; not the quietness that comes from lack of noise, but the quietness that comes from the absence of distraction. God took my sense of detachment from the world, created by my foster care experience, and turned it into a calling. My pain was transformed in the fires of providence, into a resolve to pursue a life of quiet reflection, a scholarly life that would require money, effort and education if it were to become a reality.

It was at Angelus Temple that I met Christy, my first college girlfriend. Circumstances found us riding in the same car to church on Sundays. Sometimes she and her friend Sue would invite me over for lunch at the place they stayed in the afternoons, and gradually we got to know each other. Christy had long blond hair and an attractive figure, not thin, but shapely in a way that commanded attention. She was very bubbly and talkative, but didn't seem to mind my quiet manner. In fact, I noticed that as time passed I was getting more and more invitations to spend the afternoons with her and Sue.

I developed a fondness for Christy, but was unsure of her feelings toward me. Then, one evening after church, we were sitting with a group at the local Denny's in Glendale, where we often met up with friends. We were all sitting around chatting as usual, and Christy was sitting beside me, when out of the blue I felt her knee brushing up against my leg. For the remainder of the meal I sat there in stunned silence, trying to appear nonchalant, as Christy made her feelings for me transparent.

Before long we were "a couple." It was near the end of the school year, and we spent as much time together as we could before parting for the summer. During the intervening months, while I was up in Salmon working to secure funds for another year of college, we exchanged phone calls and letters, which I eagerly awaited in Bud and Jan's mailbox.

Christy taught me a lot about romantic relationships. I learned to tune in to her insecurities, how to deal with occasional disagreements that surfaced, how to encourage her, when I needed to make her laugh. When the following school year started, in the fall of 1991, we continued our romance with enthusiasm, spending every possible moment together in the evenings. By this time we had both moved out of the college dorms and were living with roommates in the same apartment complex near the campus.

And then, as suddenly as it had started, something just, changed. I began to feel uneasy with the prospect of a long-term commitment to Christy, as pretty and sweet as she was. One of my roommates at that time, Craig Kulonis, had a terrible crush on her that had a long history, and maybe that made me uncomfortable. I don't know. But I began to feel trapped by her affection, and started coming up with excuses as to why I couldn't spend time with her. Soon the inevitable happened, and one warm California evening, sometime around late September, we went out for a walk. I explained to her that I thought it would be best if we stopped seeing each other for awhile. Her eyes filled up with tears and she nodded her head in brave acceptance.

"I need to go," she said, turning from me and pulling away her hands.

As I watched her walk away and out of my life, I felt a tremendous rush of relief and regret in one awful moment, as I gained my freedom at her expense. In the end though, it turned out for the best. Soon thereafter, Christy began dating my lovesick roommate Craig, and they eventually married.

Not long after I broke up with Christy, I began dating Delinda. I can still recall the first time I saw her, two years prior. It was at the old Echo Park campus, and she was wandering around the college bookstore with her mother. She was short, thin and wiry, with athletic features, yet she carried herself with such poise that she made her tomboy appearance look elegant. Like a Jack Russell Terrier, bouncing on its toes. Her hair was blond, of medium length, going down to the neckline. I didn't say a word to her, but often noticed her distracting presence at chapel services. One day I worked up the courage to speak with her outside in the courtyard, and she invited me to go to the beach with her and her friends. She had my heart at that point.

The following year, I decided to talk to her about my feelings, which had not abated over the summer. I knocked on her door at the girls' dorm and waited for her to appear. The door opened, and there she was, standing there, dressed in shorts and a t-shirt, no makeup. I had to force my voice box to work.

"Hey Delinda," I said, trying to be calm. "Do you have a minute to talk?"

"Sure," she replied, no doubt knowing why I was there and trying to hide it. "Let me go put some shoes on." After a few moments of hidden conversation with her roommate, she reappeared. She closed the door behind her and we walked outside.

After some small talk I made my confession. "I've been meaning to talk to you for awhile now about something I've been struggling with," I began. "I don't know if you've noticed, but I really like you, a lot. I guess I'm just wondering what you think about me, and if you feel the same way. Or…"

I waited for her to finish my thought, hopefully affirming that yes, she shared my romantic feelings. She looked back at me mercifully though, the way a hunter looks with empathy at a fallen deer before administering a final shot.

"You don't know how flattered I am to hear you say that," she began. "And I'm so glad you shared it with me. But actually, I feel that way about somebody else right now, and I'm trying to figure out how I'm going to tell him what you're telling me. So I know how hard it is for you."

Not being able to locate a hole to sink into, I endured a few more minutes of tortuous conversation before parting paths with a painful hug. Shortly thereafter, she began dating a tall basketball player, appropriately named Doug (he looked like a Doug), who played the drums for the college worship team during chapel services. He was also a star on the college basketball team. How could I compete with that? Soon they were engaged, though later on they broke up over something to do with one of Doug's old girlfriends.

My contacts with Delinda had remained casual but constant since that time, through classes and our church attendance at Angelus Temple. One day out of the blue, after Christy and I broke up, she came over to me outside of class, and invited me to sit with her the next time I came to church. I felt more at home, more stable and secure sitting next to Delinda in church than I had felt since the death of my mother. I discovered a pretty girl who cares about you can heal your soul.

The romance lasted from October until January. We broke up for the first time in December, before I left for Idaho at the Christmas break. I was over at her place, and she began expressing to me her feelings about the hopelessness of our future. I would be attending graduate school when I finished college, whereas she was going to be returning to Brazil, where she was raised, to work with homeless children. Plus, I was a bookish scholar-in-the-making, whereas she could care less about books and studying. She just didn't think it would work out. We were sitting in the dining area of her apartment as she broke the news to me, on stools, facing each other alongside the kitchen counter. I grew quiet, and she asked me what I was thinking.

"I'm thinking that I didn't want things to end this way," I replied.

She moved closer to me and said, "I know, neither did I."

Then, for some reason, she pulled me up against her, and the next thing I knew we were a mass of flesh, kissing one another with a passion that had somehow been sparked by the prospect of breaking up. But it was not to last. The next time she worked up the courage to call it quits, after we had returned from the Christmas break, she broke it to me over the phone.

The following fall of 1992, after months of separation, she again had a change of heart. She called me on the phone at my apartment and asked if we could go get a coffee at the local donut shop. There she confessed to me that she thought she had made a mistake, and wanted us to try to work things out. Perhaps we could stay in California until I finished graduate school, or maybe she would go to Brazil first, while I worked on my master's degree, and then I could join her and we would marry. Surely we could make *something* work. We played out different scenarios.

We were still tied to one another emotionally, though the prospect of our sharing a common future was, realistically, slim to none. So we pretended for the time being. Now and then she suggested that I should consider putting off graduate school, go work with her in Brazil, and return to my studies later on. But the more she talked this way, the more it became clear that we were doomed.

I loved Delinda, but I knew that my whole life had been preparing me for something, some calling of God upon my existence. If I did not go on to further academic studies, my soul would shrivel up and I would die, knowing I had never lived up to my obligations, my potential place of service within the fabric of this world. So one evening I went over to Delinda's apartment, spoke with her outside, and told her that though I would always care deeply for her, there was no way we could ever be together in the long run. So, we might as well accept that and move on. Once we had both shared our feelings, she finally signaled her acceptance with a shrug of the shoulders, simply saying "Okay."

I walked away, knowing I had done the right thing, and wondering still if that is what I should have done.

Does doing the right thing always result in maximal happiness in this life?

Some months later, in the spring of 1993, I met up with Delinda in Glendale, where we said our final goodbyes. I was getting ready to graduate from college. She was scheduled to fly to Brazil the following day, to join her parents at their orphanage, working with the poorest of God's street children.

It was during the spring rains, and the storms beat down on the windows of the restaurant where we sat for our final meal together. She talked with excitement about the future and her burden for the poor and the outcast. I sat there trying to think of some scenario whereby I could join her, or some way of talking her out of getting on that damn plane. I pretended to listen, but the only sound I could hear was the breaking of my heart, and the despair that comes from the finality of goodbye. I knew I would never see her again.

Before I could formulate a plan, I was again parked outside the house in Glendale where she was staying. The wind and rain were battering furiously against the windows of my car as she got ready to open the door and run inside, running away from me and out of my life forever. I looked over at her and could see tears welling up in her eyes. There was nothing to be said really.

We embraced and she muttered in my ear with a sniffle, "I'm gonna miss you." With that, she kissed me on the cheek and was gone. I aimed the car through the darkness, and soon was back on the LA freeways, embracing fate, driving through the rain, through the pain, wiping away the tears, so I could see the way forward, toward the east, toward my own future.

Wandering in the Desert (1993-1995)

As May of 1993 approached, my plans for graduate school began to take shape. After studying the programs of many of the leading seminaries across the country, ranging from Fuller in California to Gordon-Conwell in Massachusetts, I settled on Dallas Theological Seminary in the center of the nation. Dallas combined high academic standards with conservative theological scholarship, and that is what I was looking for at the time. Many of the faculty members at DTS were familiar to me through my classroom texts and lectures.

One of my favorite pastimes on Saturdays was to hang out at the local Christian bookstore in West Covina. I spent hours in their used book section, browsing the shelves and drinking the free coffee. It was around this time that somebody at the bookstore introduced me to a local man named Robert Frost. Robert was a graduate of DTS from the early 1980's, and an avid lay-scholar. He made a living through computer programming and maintenance for a company in Pasadena, but spent all his spare time studying Greek and Hebrew, and staying abreast of the latest biblical scholarship. I took an immediate liking to

Robert. He was short and muscular, built an awful lot like Don Brown from my previous life, with graying brown hair. He had intelligent eyes, and a serious expression which resonated with me, as it was a lot like my own. We instantly hit it off.

By the end of our first visit I had an invitation to join him and his family at his home for dinner, which I gratefully accepted. A few days later I found myself pulling my car up to their home in Glendora. It was of modest size, located at the end of a pleasant cul-de-sac in a safe suburban neighborhood. I sat down that evening to a plate of pasta, washed down by plentiful supplies of cold milk, surrounded by the table-chatter of Robert and his family. I quickly grew fond of the Frosts, and before long I was making weekly visits to their house for dinner on weekends. We never ran out of topics for discussion, ranging from my college coursework, to my plans for attending DTS and what I might expect there, to an endless variety of theological subjects.

We also talked about ourselves, our stories, our personal journeys. Robert grew up as a nominal Roman Catholic in Colorado, served in the Navy in Vietnam, became an evangelical Christian in his twenties after a period of religious skepticism, and had a lot of interesting life stories. His pretty wife Vicki sat quietly during my visits, listening to our banter. She enjoyed sitting back and watching as Robert turned the clock back on his aging process. She always made me feel welcome in their home, as did their three girls (ranging in age from eight to thirteen). I began attending church with them on Sundays, attracted by the fact that their pastor was pursuing a doctor of ministry degree at DTS at that time. His course of study required him to fly to the Dallas campus regularly for seminars, and he was happy to talk to me about my plans for moving and studying there.

Robert was the last in a long line of surrogate fathers with whom my path would cross. Sitting in the midst of his family, I felt like "John Boy," headed off to the big city to pursue an advanced education. Long

187

after Vicki and the girls had gone to bed, we would sit at his kitchen table over coffee and talk late into the night.

If there was a pause in the conversation, his eyes would suddenly widen and he'd say, "You want some more pasta?" It was a ploy, designed to fill the air with words, lest I prematurely come to the conclusion that it was time to go home. Robert desperately wanted my company, and I wanted him to want my company. Eventually I would stumble out to my car with sleepy eyes and drive home.

We would often meet up at McDonald's or one of the other local cafes in the neighborhood, and talk about whatever was on our minds at the moment. The topic didn't matter. As time went on he shared deeply personal things with me about his life, and his struggles, things I could not share with others. I was like a priest I suppose, someone upon whom he could unload the burdens of his deepest self without fear of rejection or judgment.

As I was preparing to move to Dallas, my old AMC Concord finally stopped running. Money was tight, and I wondered how I was going to purchase another car. Robert stepped in and offered me his old El Camino, a big, tan beast with a rumbling engine, which seemed to run reliably. I graciously accepted his gift, and my car problem was solved. When the time came to go to Dallas, Robert rode all the way with me, so that I did not have to make that first journey by myself.

Together we drove through the hot California deserts, across the parched lands of New Mexico, and into the vast plains of the Texas countryside, until we arrived, weary but safe, in Dallas. Along the way we stopped now and then to eat or nap or go to the bathroom, as men do when they need a break from driving, standing at the side of the road, feeling alive. One of my enduring memories will always be of Robert, there at the wheel (lacking confidence in my driving), and the hot desert air blowing in through the windows, carrying the two of us as into the vast unknown of my adventure.

I attended Dallas Seminary for one year. I successfully tested out of the introductory Greek language courses and (a little proudly) went straight into the second year. I thoroughly enjoyed studying biblical literature and theology under some of the world's finest evangelical scholars. The research facilities there were world-class, and I spent countless hours in the seminary library, moving from shelf to shelf, eagerly snatching books like a child in a candy store. I quickly found a job working at the warehouse of an office furniture company, which paid $9 an hour, which sufficed to get me through the year financially, alongside my student loans.

Isolated from my previous college environment, and lacking the nurture of Robert's family, I felt very isolated that year. My memories are full of scenes that give expression to the restlessness that followed me everywhere. Driving by myself in the car in the Texas heat, listening to music to fill the empty space with a voice; visiting various churches and bookstores week by week, hoping to meet people; missing Delinda (with whom I exchanged letters that year until she announced she had met another man); driving to work in the winter in my freezing El Camino with no heat; coming back to the campus library after a shift at work, struggling with my waning enthusiasm; listening to the stories of other lonely, single seminary students, whose attention was divided between the pursuit of education and women.

By the time the school year ended in May of 1994, I knew I needed a change of routine to keep my soul from shriveling up. I considered switching from the imposing four-year master of theology degree, to a two-year master of arts in biblical exegesis and linguistics, which seemed to suit me better. I also considered whether to just sit out a year and do something else for awhile.

That summer I drove up to Logan, Utah, to work with my old friend Ray Hedlund, who operated a small landscaping business there. My days were filled with hard labor, digging sprinkler lines, planting bushes and laying sod alongside two other young men who comprised the crew. Ray seemed to feel the need to crack the whip on me all the harder because I was his friend. He tolerated no wasted time or movement during work hours, and expected all of us to move at a frantic pace, pushing ourselves hard throughout the day under the hot Utah sun. I have always been given to daydreaming and distraction when employed in repetitious physical labor, and it didn't make for a good combination. There was a lot of tension between us at the job sites.

There were some good times too. For dinner we would either eat out at local cafes (with Ray hitting on every waitress we met), or bring home thick steaks to cook on the stove. Now and then we would take drives into the beautiful mountains around Logan, park and talk about a whole variety of matters, ranging from deer hunting, to past girlfriends, to points of theology, to strategies for Christian ministry to the Mormons all around us in Utah. (In addition to landscaping, Ray was also trying to plant a new Foursquare church in Logan.) We would often visit churches in the surrounding towns on Sunday evenings, hoping to meet single women. Ray was keen to find a wife, and I was certainly open to some female company as well. As the summer wore on though, we argued more and more frequently at home and the worksites, and I got the sense that his small home was not going to be big enough for the two of us much longer.

Looking back on it, there are a lot of possible explanations for the tensions that existed between us. I was pursuing advanced education at a famous theological seminary, whereas he was fortunate to have completed his three-year certificate program in the study of the Bible at our college. If I became a college professor, I would enter a comfortable middle-class lifestyle, while he seemed destined to struggle on the edges of poverty, working a full-time job of hard labor, while trying to establish a fruitful church ministry on the side.

Ray was in his mid-thirties, with no prospect of marriage. I still

190

had youth on my side at least. My presence in Ray's home may have highlighted not only his lack of worldly success, but the lack of a wife. I was reserving the space set aside for her. My being there reminded him of who was still *not* there. Or maybe, at the end of the day, perhaps I was simply a pain to live with, and annoyed him in ways that were and are beyond my ability to analyze.

Toward the end of the summer I received an invitation from one of my former professors, to come out to Quartz Hill, California (about 90 minutes to the north of Los Angeles) and work with the college ministry at his church. Having determined that another year of struggling at DTS was more than I could bear, I jumped at the opportunity. When August rolled around, I gladly said goodbye to Ray while we still had a friendship, and headed back down to Dallas to collect my things. Then I would turn around and make my way back to southern California.

My trip down to Dallas was relaxing. I was greeted with beautiful summer scenery as I traveled down the open freeway, making my way through Wyoming and Colorado, down into New Mexico, moving south toward Texas. I drove with the windows down, allowing the smell of sagebrush to fill my car. I remember stopping at a small hotel somewhere south of Colorado Springs, and relaxing outside after a filling café meal as the sun crept down the horizon, struck by the peaceful beauty around me, feeling positive. I was lonely, but it was a serene kind of loneliness that was full of possibility in the face of an open future.

Sometime the next day I made my way through Texas. I remember stopping somewhere along the 20 freeway west of Dallas late in the afternoon, and ordering a meal at a folksy truckers' restaurant. For some reason, the waitress who served me caught my attention. She was tall and athletic, with long blond hair, strong legs and a motherly bearing. She had that simple sort of feminine charm that you often find in waitresses, a plain sort of understated beauty. I was curious.

How did she end up working all the way out here, in the middle of nowhere, lost somewhere in the vastness of the quiet Texas plains? Had she gone to school near here? Seeing no wedding ring on her hand, as I sipped my coffee I wondered if she had once been married to a man from this area, and after they separated, she just decided to stay put. If I were still living in Dallas, I thought to myself, I might be tempted to drive back out here and order another hot meal, just to get another chance to visit with her. It wasn't really that far of a drive after all. What a charming and simple life it would be, to live out here, in the quiet countryside, falling in love, enjoying the company of such a woman.

It was obvious that at age twenty-three, I was missing some social necessity, something fundamental at the seat of my soul, company that no library could replace. At the end of the day, what man would not trade all the books in the world for the love of a woman, the sort of woman who can compel you to sit down with her over a cup of coffee and hear her life story? I left the restaurant, having barely spoken a word to the waitress, leaving her with no idea of the spell she had cast on me. The fact was, of course, I would not be returning to see her, for my path was taking me back to California. So I wished her a wordless farewell, and traveled on.

I wonder if she still works there at that café, serving up orders to dusty truck drivers even as I type these words.

My arrival in Dallas went smoothly enough. I went back to the seminary dorm, gathered up my things, and turned around the next day to venture back west. However, no sooner had I gotten outside of the city when I began to notice the car was acting strangely. My inexperience with mechanical issues gave me little understanding of the problem, but soon it became obvious that my El Camino was overheating. The car began to slow down, and I pulled off of the side of the road near a truck stop just as it boiled over. I asked a friendly bystander for advice, and he told me I would need to buy some coolant for the car's radiator. Thus began a long and painful journey from Dallas to Los Angeles, stopping to allow the car to cool off every couple of hours, replacing the coolant liquid, and journeying on until I broke down again. It was a stressful, miserable way to travel through the deserts of the southwest.

I was slowly making my way along the next day, when somewhere to the west of Albuquerque I got a flat tire. I managed to pull the car off the road, onto land belonging to an Indian reservation. All my earthly possessions were in the back of that El Camino, yet I had no choice but to leave it behind and hitchhike back into town for a tire. I walked for a long time along the 40 freeway, humiliated, putting out my thumb as cars drove by, only to watch them whiz past me. Finally, some kind person, hauling boxes of fruit in a pickup truck, stopped and offered me a lift. He drove me back into Albuquerque and dropped me off at a hotel.

I would need to stay there for the night, until the tire store opened the next morning. I ordered a meal at a local café, and returned to my lonely quarters. I turned on the TV and sat there on the bed, pondering my fate in my hotel room. I was rapidly running out of money. The trip was taking more time than I had anticipated. And I was utterly alone. I now regretted my decision to take a year out of seminary. Perhaps this was all a sign that I belonged in the safe halls of academia, not on my own in the harshness of the outside world, with no support.

I was back at Harbor House, with nobody to call. I had no parents who would take any interest if I told them I was stranded in the middle of New Mexico, running out of money. I could call Bud and Jan, but they would tell me there was nothing they could do. I knew I had an uncle in Los Alamos, but I hadn't spoken to him in years. Robert and Vicki had already done more to help me than I had any right to expect.

The next morning I began calling local churches in town, hoping at least for a ride back to my car with the tire, only to be told time and again by church secretaries and pastors alike, that they were not in any position to offer help. Finally, one Assemblies of God church told me there was a person in their congregation who might be able to offer assistance. If I left them my number, they would have him call me. Later that day, he called, and agreed to take me to my car, after verifying my identity and driver's license information. He was a small man, with a balding head and glasses, who looked to be of mixed Hispanic descent perhaps. He was very business-like, wary of being conned or lured into the snare of a serial killer, but at least he was offering me a ride.

After a trip to a tire store, the man dropped me off back at the Indian reservation. The sky was threatening rain, and we replaced the flat tire just as the heavy drops began to descend upon us. With a courteous handshake and a wish of good luck, he was gone. None of my possessions had been bothered by the locals. I had seen a few of their humble houses from the road. I wondered about them and their lives.

My lonely travels made me long for connections. Maybe, living in their midst on this land would be a better option than continuing on my journey to California. I was suddenly jealous of the black-haired people I saw in the distance, traveling along the road, riding their bikes, mingling around their small homes without a care in the world. At least they had a place to stay when the sun set, a space to call their own, even if it was in the middle of the desert. I traveled on.

It took me another couple of days before I crawled into the Los Angeles area. I had memorable breakdowns along the way, in Flagstaff, Arizona, and Needles, California, among other sites of less renown. I remember Flagstaff distinctly, for I was struck by the beauty. I remember sitting outside a convenience store in Flagstaff, looking up and down what appeared to be the main drag, while waiting for my car to cool off, and thinking how nice it would be to settle down here and make a home in such an idyllic setting.

The pine trees and forests in the area created a sense of nearness to wilderness that calms the soul. The area reminded me in some ways of

Mack's Inn, where I had enjoyed such pleasant times with Mac and my mother in another world. It wasn't really that long ago, when majestic grizzly bears would have haunted those mountains.

I think often of the fate of the grizzly in the southwest. As the 20th century dawned, they became a tribe without a home. Driven from their quiet mountain ranges by settlers, ranchers and government trappers, they fled to the remotest wilderness. Looking for solitary places, free from intrusion, places of belonging, where they would not be treated as trespassers. With each passing decade their space became more crowded, until finally, in the 30's and 40's, they vanished. By the 1950's there were no more of these predators stalking the mountains of the southwest, save a few lonely stragglers in the remotest parts of southern Colorado.

But did we really kill off the grizzlies? Or is it they, repulsed by our lack of reverence, who abandoned us to our empty, murderous existence? Do their ghosts still wander the wild, quiet places of the southwest, hidden safely from bullets, traps and heartless men?

I broke down again in Needles, and my miseries were compounded when I locked my keys in the car while venturing into McDonald's for some refreshment. So I had to spend more of my dwindling cash for AAA service. While waiting inside the McDonald's for the sun to go down, for cooler temperatures to travel, I sat and listened with disbelief as some fool shared with his two friends a ghoulish story of a dog he had witnessed being beaten to death with a tire iron.

"So he's fuckin' freakin' out, cause no matter how many times he hits this dog, it just keeps fuckin' howling."

They chuckled, insipid smirks on their soulless, smudgy faces.

How does a man witness such a thing, and then go to sleep at night?

Does he sleep at night at all?

I broke down again in the mountains west of Needles, and it was only through some mechanical assistance offered by a group of rednecks, who looked like they belonged to a motorcycle gang, that I managed to make it safely to Glendora. I spent a day or so with Robert and Vicki, telling them my tales of woe, before completing the last leg of my trip to Quartz Hill. I arrived there, stressed, weary and poor, but in one piece.

Unfortunately, my move to Quartz Hill was a disappointment. Though the pastor of the church had agreed over the phone, to pay my traveling expenses, when I brought up the subject upon my arrival, he now claimed to know of no such agreement. Since I was nearly broke, he agreed to provide some financial help—but I would need to pay it back of course. Sigh. *Where do these pastors come from anyways?*

As my compensation for working with the church's college group, and tending the grounds (watering trees, cleaning, painting, etc.), it was agreed that I would be allowed to stay in one of the empty apartments the church owned. But that promise never materialized either, and (after a brief stay at the pastor's luxurious home) I was moved into one of the back rooms of the building where the church's junior high group met. It was the sort of room where you would store odds and ends that you didn't know where else to put, and apparently it was viewed as appropriate housing for me.

I stayed there in Quartz Hill, working without pay for that church, for about six months. I wandered in the wilderness, like the Israelites in the Bible. My tenure as the college worker only lasted a couple of months. Then I was abruptly relieved of my duties. I had no idea how to disciple and entertain a group of students not that much younger than myself, but my sudden termination was discouraging. I was given no reason, but was simply told by the pastor that the arrangement wasn't "working out."

This meant that my "churchly" duties were maintaining the ground facilities. For spending money, I got a job with a local landscaping company, putting to work some of the skills I had learned the previous summer working for Ray. I quickly became adept at installing sprinkler systems in the housing subdivisions popping up like rabbits all over the area. I would install sprinkler systems by day, come home and tend to the church grounds for an hour or two, and then spend lonely evenings drinking coffee and reading at the local cafes. It was a time of searching, roaming aimlessly through the passing weeks, trying to figure out where I fit in, what direction my life was heading. My daily routine was simple. Driving around to job sites, stopping for lunch at fast food restaurants, listening to the radio as I rode in my old car. In a strange sort of way, the dullness was alluring.

For a few weeks I struck up a relationship with a woman in the church named Julie, to whom I was introduced by some well-meaning match-makers. She was a single mother with two young boys. She had long, blond hair, pretty blue eyes, and a gorgeous figure. We got along well, and she soon expressed to me the belief that I was just the sort of man she had been looking for. She confided that until fairly recently she had been employed as *a stripper* of all things, though now she had found God and was trying to walk a different path. I pondered the possibility of abandoning academia. Why not just continue with landscaping, settle down with her, and help to raise her children?

But then, suddenly, she cooled off. She said she needed some time to herself, and that this was not the right time for her to pursue a romantic relationship with anyone. The next thing I heard, she had reunited with her ex-husband, a local bail bondsman of somewhat notorious character. I returned to my routine of isolation, spending my evenings in the smoky booths of the rustic diners I frequented. I was saddened by the loneliness that now reentered my life, but I was more haunted by the thoughts of her returning to a life that she told me had caused her misery. I hope her story took a positive turn.

Then, something happened early in 1995 that set me on a different course. The pastor decided they did not want me living in the junior high youth building anymore. They needed the space for some other purpose. So it was determined that I would be moved in with another single man in the congregation, with whom I was casually acquainted, who lived in an old house that the church happened to own.

At first I accepted the change in arrangements. I loaded up my cargo into the back of my El Camino and drove over to the house. As I started to unload my belongings, the man who lived there was pacing back and forth between the kitchen and the living room. *"I told them* I didn't want anyone living with me," he announced in a hostile tone as I came through the door. I looked at him, and was taken aback by his dark scowl. He was an odd man, around fifty years of age, who seemed to wear camouflage most of the time. An airplane mechanic by trade. There was something about his sulking manner that made me uneasy. I did not feel safe going to sleep in that house with him in the room next door.

That was enough. I had spent too many years of my life, moving around from place to place, living with people who did not desire my presence. At the age of 24, it was more than I could bear. I called Robert and Vicki and explained to them my situation. For months, they had been encouraging me to get out of there, and relocate to Glendora with them. They were more than happy to allow me to stay in their spare room, and they offered to help me purchase a reliable vehicle to replace my dying El Camino.

"What you need to do is get back into graduate school," Robert had repeatedly counseled me. Now I took his advice.

The Road to Scotland (1995-1997)

Once I had agreed to take Robert and Vicki up on their offer, I wasted no time in extracting myself from my situation in Quartz Hill. The next day I met with the pastor in his office and told him I had decided to leave, having given only six months of my agreed year of service. He offered no arguments, and seemed more than happy to be rid of me. My arrangement with the church had proved disappointing from both ends, and we gladly parted ways. I then handed in my resignation to the landscaping company I was working for, which ironically seemed to cause much more disappointment to my secular employers. They genuinely liked me and were sad to see me go.

A few days later, I loaded up my sick old El Camino and drove out of the high deserts of the Palmdale area, through the mountain passes above Pasadena (where some of the last holdouts of the California grizzly population had sought refuge only a few generations earlier), and down into the San Gabriel valley, which I was now to call home. I found a job at a local car repossession business in Pomona, working in the office, answering phones and dealing with an irate public.

My choices of graduate school boiled down to Fuller Theological Seminary in Pasadena and Biola University's graduate school of theology. After comparing the costs and programs of both institutions, I decided to apply for the master's in New Testament studies at Biola. As the fall term drew near, I quit my job with the repossession agency, and took a job closer to the campus, as a sales clerk at a Christian bookstore in Whittier.

My first year at Biola (1995-1996) was a positive and rewarding time. With Robert and Vicki's help, I purchased a little blue Nissan pickup truck for $2,000, which I loved to drive. It was the first vehicle I owned that I actually looked forward to driving, and it never broke down. I would leave from Glendora early in the morning while it was still dark, and take the quiet back streets through the hills of Hacienda Heights, ambling down into Whittier on the way to La Mirada, taking time to sit in the university parking lot with a hot cup of coffee before classes.

Carl Mosser, a friend and former roommate from college, enrolled at Talbot at the same time, and our friendship deepened and blossomed as we shared classes and experiences that year. He too had grown up in Idaho, under difficult circumstances, and he too had found in academia a path of escape from the hopelessness of the past. New vistas of religious scholarship opened up to us as we learned and studied together. We both became deeply interested in extracanonical Jewish literature, and scrambled together enough money to fund a trip to Brigham Young University the following summer to attend a scholarly conference on the Dead Sea Scrolls.

My second year in grad school (1996-1997) involved some awkward transitions. Early in 1996, the Frosts brought home a puppy for me from the pet store, a delightful 7-week old Staffordshire Bull Terrier-mix. (Mac had died in Idaho under mysterious circumstances in the summer of 1992 while in the care of the Lockes.) I was delighted by the surprise, and named the new puppy Candi. I loved sleeping with her on my bed when she was little, drawing comfort from the warmth of her little body through the night. But as she grew, Vicki insisted she start sleeping in the kennel outdoors, which set in motion a series of events that brought about an end of my stay there.

Left to herself out in the kennel, Candi took to barking loudly early in the mornings, which brought complaints from the neighbors. The Frosts received a written warning from the animal control authorities, and Vicki began to hint to me that Candi's presence was a problem.

"You're going to have to do something with her, or find another place to stay. We can't have the neighbors complaining about us."

Faced with the prospect of having to get rid of my new dog, I decided to move out, by this time under rather stressful circumstances. I located a room to rent in a house where I could keep Candi, with a group of Latino bachelors in Los Angeles, a few blocks from the USC campus. My living quarters were dirty and humble, and I had no connection to my Hispanic housemates. They allowed me to keep Candi, but insisted that she stay outdoors; not my preference, but I had no choice.

Once again, I found myself frustrated by my inability to care for the life entrusted to me, a mirror of my own experience in the world of foster care. Candi was adept at escaping from the yard out of boredom, and I came home one afternoon to discover that she had been hit by a car. The vet bill cost me around a thousand dollars at a time when I had little money to my name. My failure to take proper care of Candi wore on my psyche, reminding me of the guilt I felt as I saw the way Mac had to live. I knew all too well what it felt like to be on the receiving end of negligence.

During that period, I suffered from an agonizing spiritual struggle. I felt lonely and lost. I felt like I ought to be somewhere, though I wasn't sure where. I struggled with a general malaise that I could not put my finger on. I continued to attend evangelical congregations on Sundays, but somehow it didn't seem to be working anymore. Something was missing. I even found myself being drawn back to the Mormon Church. I met on a weekly basis with the LDS Institute director at USC. The director chatted with me, answered my probing questions, and asked some of his own, encouraging my search without attempting to take advantage of my vulnerability.

To this day, when I think of the Mormon Church, I think of community, families, people who stick together. I think of my ancestors, like Brigham Young, and see wagon trains of Mormon settlers making their way westward, searching for a home to call their own. I see quiet farming communities in southern Idaho, places like Teton, Roberts, Rigby, and Blackfoot, engaging in their monastic-like rhythms despite the busy world. I envision Christmas plays, women in pretty dresses, Sunday school songs for little children, men dressed in their Sunday best. I always see it from the outside, looking in through the window. Always looking in, never entering. Admiring, envious of what I see, and yet still a skeptic of Joseph Smith and his story. Conscious that somehow I just will never fit in, and am not meant to.

I spent Christmas morning of 1996 eating a breakfast meal at McDonald's so that my housemates would not have to feel sorry for me, hiding from the world's celebrations and family gatherings. I brought home a chunk of my sausage biscuit for Candi, and we quietly spent the rest of the day together. I was keenly conscious of my lack of ties to the outside world, my separation from the bulk of humanity, the absence of family and a supportive community in my life. The darkness before the dawn.

I was about to go to places I never would have imagined. While my life was full of loneliness and disappointment, my academic successes were now getting the attention of my professors at Biola. I was getting ready to graduate in the spring and wasn't sure what I should do. One afternoon, I sat down with Dr. Clint Arnold to discuss the options ahead of me. He felt sure I would be well suited for doctoral studies, a necessary step for any aspiring scholar who desires to teach for a profession. While discussing some of the possibilities over a meal on campus, he paused, chewing on his sandwich.

"Have you thought about Edinburgh? Larry Hurtado just moved over there from the University of Manitoba, and he would make a wonderful supervisor."

That very afternoon I did a bit of research, and discovered that Hurtado's specialization was in the area of non-canonical Jewish literature written prior to the New Testament, precisely the religious terrain I was most interested in exploring. I wrote him a letter and dropped it in the mailbox, describing to him my interest in Jewish apocalyptic literature and some possible research topics. He promptly replied with a promising letter of his own. With his encouragement, I applied to the doctoral program in the department of New Testament Language, Literature and Theology, at the University of Edinburgh in Scotland.

After a couple months of anxious waiting, in the spring of 1997 I received a letter in the mail from the university. I knew that sealed envelope would determine what direction the future was to take me. I nervously opened the letter, sitting under the heat of the sun on the front porch steps of that old house. I could scarcely believe what my eyes read. An invitation into the PhD program was being extended to me! My poor mother had always dreamed of finishing high school. What would she think of her son attending one of the oldest, most prestigious research universities in all of Europe? Candi was sitting beside me on the steps, watching me. I hugged her neck, knowing that my way forward would come at the expense of our special bond.

All the pain, rejection, and humiliation of the previous fourteen years was erased—if but for a moment—from my consciousness. No amount of past misery could outweigh the privilege which was now being extended to me. I looked around me at the miserable scenery of inner city LA. Not my home for much longer. In the following weeks, I was blessed to find a dog-loving co-worker from the bookstore where I worked, who agreed to take Candi home with her to stay in her family's spacious house (where she would live indoors and happy). And I booked a one-way ticket to Scotland.

In the summer of 1997, after I graduated from Biola, an interesting religious impulse took root. Not far from where I lived near USC was a large Episcopalian church. It was a grand and imposing piece of stone architecture, and for some reason its serene grey presence, which I had been blithely driving past for months on my way to McDonalds, now began to draw me in. After a decade of journeying, the glibness of my evangelical experience (with all the good intentions) was no longer adequate for my spiritual needs. I needed a church more deeply rooted, and liturgical. I began reading about Anglican theology and worship. I attended the Sunday morning Mass at an Episcopalian church, and visited with the resident priest after the service. The one, holy, catholic and apostolic Church was calling me home.

In September of 1997, I said goodbye to my old friend Carl at the LAX airport. "Good luck," he said. "Shown 'em what us boys from Idaho are made of." He would eventually follow me to the UK, securing a place in a doctoral program at the University of St. Andrews a few years later.

After checking my luggage, I made my way to the gate and boarded a non-stop flight from L.A. to London, making a connection there to Edinburgh. I sat down in my seat and looked around me at my fellow passengers. Their journeys had taken them through the paths of their own stories, yet in this pregnant moment, all our roads were intersecting. For the next twelve hours or so, they would be my community. I was not alone. I leaned back contentedly against the headrest, and looked to the side, where I could gaze out the window toward the west.

The sun was just setting, announcing the conclusion of the day with a dramatic display of color and beauty. It was the last American sunset I would be seeing for a while. I had no idea where my path would ultimately lead, but I sensed in that poignant moment, the sign of a turning point. The sunset was a token of the conclusion of my wandering. From now on I would go, not where cruelty, chance and misfortune took me captive, but where my gifts, initiative and opportunities directed. I closed my eyes and said a silent prayer of thanks to God as the aircraft left the runway and moved forward at awesome speeds, soaring above the clouds, into the horizon of the future.

Epilogue

More than a decade has passed since that flight to Scotland. I write these words from the comforts of my modest home in western North Carolina. In Scotland, I met my wife Alice, who traveled with me to America when I accepted my first job, teaching Greek and biblical literature in the religion department of Montreat College, nestled in the Blue Ridge Mountains near Asheville.

Our lifestyle is comfortable, though by no means wealthy. I prepare classroom lectures, serve on committees, advise students in their academic programs. Now and then I publish books and articles in the field of religion, though I am far from prolific. We have four dogs, all of whom live indoors with us and are spoiled beyond belief. It is enough. Perhaps that is why I'm here on this earth at the end of the day. I know what is important to have.

I often think about my past, especially my mother. She struggled with difficult fortunes. Physical handicaps and other circumstances limited her options. But she had a son, and she did her best to raise him with the resources she had at her disposal. Maybe at times her efforts seemed futile. Yet if the success of a mother is measured by the capacity of her child to survive the stormy chaos of life, she seems to have done something right. Though she is long gone, I am still here. I live and breathe and write. I carry her memory in my thoughts throughout my days. I see her in my psyche, my mannerisms, and the traits of my unique personality.

Do any of us truly know what successes we might be unwittingly bequeathing upon the world?

Can any of us imagine what futures we create just by our being here and playing our part, and by our simple choices?

The other characters in my story lie strewn, like fallen warriors, across the battleground of my consciousness. I was forced to leave Mac in the care of my foster parents when I went away to college. The Summers soon grew weary of caring for him, and I turned to the Lockes for help. They then allowed him to run unrestrained around the countryside until one day his body was found on a neighboring property, cause of death suspicious, but unknown (to me at least). I feel a deep guilt over the way Mac's life ended, that I will take with me to my grave. He was the saddest casualty of my foster care.

I don't know what became of Jean Pugh, and Richard and Betty Moore. I heard years ago that Jean had retired and moved out East. The members of the Eagle Rock Kennel Club, who fostered my love of the dog fancy, have scattered to the winds. Now and then I come across one or another of them on the Internet, as they continue to run the show circuits. Their club still meets in Idaho Falls, as does the Upper Snake River Valley Dog Training Club.

Bonnie and Norman Hunting live in a trailer near Rigby, Idaho. I hear they enjoy camping and visiting Island Park on the weekends. As to what became of Keith Birch, I have no idea. I ran into him at a family picnic in 1997, just before I left for Scotland, as I visited people in Idaho one more time. Somebody asked him if he recognized me, and he said,

"Hell yes. I was half-tempted to walk over and slap him upside his head just for old time's sake." Later I heard, he and Sandy divorced.

Lance and Janice Whitmore still live in La Grande, Oregon. Their sons Jesse and Tony have lives that are cluttered with the effects of bad choices. Lance, Jr. left the logging career handed down from his father, causing no small amount of tension. I have hardly spoken with them since I left, though I do hear from Mitch now and then by email.

Don Brown was shot and killed in West Virginia, about 10 years after I left him standing in the airport, by the woman he left Geraldine for. The woman then killed herself, leaving the whole situation in a shroud of mystery, but that's what they tell me. Geraldine continues to live in the Currituck area, and married a man who treats her well. Through the Internet, I found them all a few years ago, and got in touch. I try to visit them at least once a year. Her daughters Liz and Eileen are both married with children, and also live in the region.

Ruth Hudson died while I was in Scotland. I wrote her an email in her last days, which was read aloud to her on her death bed. She died in the love of God, in the Catholic faith, with no animosity between us.

Jim and Bonnie Lockes continue to live on their ranch in Leadore. Bud and Jan Summers are semi-retired in Salmon. Though we used to stay in contact, eventually as the years passed, the momentum of our relationships was overcome by time, and we have lost touch. They have their families to concern themselves with, and I have mine. Their unwillingness to look after Mac properly when I left for college remains a sore spot for me. It created a distance between us that will never be bridged. As to what became of the Mayers, I don't know. I know at one point they relocated to Boise, where Lee took up work as a construction laborer.

I reconciled with the Frosts before I went away to Scotland. A few years later, Robert died suddenly of a heart attack just before I came back. His wife Vicki has happily remarried from what I heard, though we have since lost touch.

As I think back on my life, I sometimes ask myself how I survived. A couple of things come to mind. I was blessed with the love of my mother in my early years. She showed me every day that I mattered to her. Had my first thirteen years not been shaped by her kindness, I might well have lacked the inner resources to survive the challenges life in foster care threw at me.

Thank you mom. I miss you.

I also had Mac. Mac gave me something to love. I remember his warm brown eyes, his soft Schnauzer mustache, and that little tongue of his, thin like bologna. Thanks to him, I had something beautiful to come home to, no matter how bad my circumstances. I have no doubt that little dog kept my soul from drying up.

Thank you Mac. I'm so sorry.

It seems to me that ordinary people can overcome extraordinary obstacles if they get just a few things right, if just a few cards fall into place for them. In my case, religious faith, and a clear direction through education, helped me on the way to a settled life. Faith gave me a taste of community, a place of belonging through the shared framework of the Christian story. My life came to be shaped by an awareness of God's presence, purpose and planning. Higher education gave me the specific direction to follow, that led me into a life of learning and purpose.

I am lucky to have found my way out of the darkness. So many young people in foster care seek community in the wrong places, and go in the wrong directions. They have no one to help them, guide them, love and nurture them. Lacking the right environment, children flounder in society, like someone in a pool who has never learned to swim.

What can we give these children so that they may grow and develop, and lead full lives?

How can we teach them to swim?

Thousands of weary foster kids are crushed every year when they are removed from failed homes and put into hopeless environments. They need to be placed with parents who can lift them up to a place of security and strength, who can polish the diamond that hides under the surface of the young who wander among us.

The significance of our lives can be measured in no better way than the impact we have on those who depend upon us. When my mother died she passed me on to the care of others, and I soon found myself among people who lacked the resources, both spiritual and financial, to help a troubled child.

What foster kids need is good news. Somebody needs to let them know that they are valuable, that their place in the complex fabric of life has meaning and dignity.

That their story, however small, is worthy of being told.

That they matter.

That they are loved.

Made in the USA
Lexington, KY
23 May 2011